NETWORKING HIGH PERFORMANCE IN NEW YORK'S SECONDARY EDUCATION

The Regents Curriculum Story

David K. Wiles

University Press of America, Inc.
Lanham • New York • London

Copyright © 1996 by
University Press of America,® Inc.
4720 Boston Way
Lanham, Maryland 20706

3 Henrietta Street
London, WC2E 8LU England

Library of Congress Cataloging-in-Publication Data

Wiles, David K.
Networking high performance in New York's secondary education :
the regents curriculum story / David K. Wiles
p.   cm.
Includes bibliographical references and index.
1. Education, Secondary--New York (State)--Curricula. 2.
Curriculum evaluation--New York (State). 3. School districts--New
York (State)--Evaluation. 4. University of the State of New York.
Regents College. 5. Social networks--New York (State). 6. Schools--
Decentralization--New York (State). 7. Academic achievement--New
York (State--Evaluation. 8. Educational accountability--New York
(State). I. Title.
LB1629.N7W45   1996   373.19'09747--dc20   95-47272 CIP

ISBN 0-7618-0236-3 (cloth: alk: ppr.)
ISBN 0-7618-0237-1 (pbk: alk: ppr.)

Contents

List of Tables

List of Figures

Introduction

During the five years this book was being prepared the core purpose for writing changed dramatically. The original intention was to describe the patterning of Regents secondary performance among New York's k-12 public school districts and suggest possibilities for collaboration in the state's commitment to improve advanced, college bound curriculums. While promoting the Regents curriculum remains a major objective, there is a new urgency suggesting the need for networking top flight, best performing school districts throughout the state.

A century old tradition of operating advanced secondary programs in New York is in real jeopardy of being transformed to the point that the vital thread of continuity with the past is lost. Further, the challenge to secondary curriculum is coupled with an attempt to dismantle the entire institutional system of public education. What was decentralization in the 1960's, devolution in the 1980's has tilted toward disintegration in the mid 1990's. Like all serious challenges, current efforts to abolish the Board of Regents and Regents secondary curriculum are not the work of wild eyed revolutionaries, nihilists or dreamers of the existential moment. Many of those who have lost faith in the capability of New York public education to rebuild upon the tradition of exemplary secondary programs are those who worked the hardest to bring such a reality about. The Pogo phrase about meeting the enemy in ourselves applies to the exhausted and angry professional educators and citizens who tried to alleviate the "at risk" conditions of the 1980's and then tried to promote the Compact for Learning intentions of this decade.

Less than a decade ago avid reformers believed that Regents authority and curricular format could contribute to the progressive evolution of public education back to its post World War Two pre-eminence as the nation's leader. Standards and curricular frameworks could provide new language for talking about improvement while site-based, teacher centered and shared decision-making suggested new forums to deliberate reform options. The important feature of thinking such new things for New York State's secondary programs was that such reform efforts would take place within the long established legacy of proven excellence and bedrock strength of the Regents format.

At mid-point in the 1990's decade, such assumptions about the intrinsic value of the Regents have been eroded. The political schisms and intellectual gulfs in current reform discussions are undeniable. Calling for the abolishment of the Board of Regents and the Regents curriculum reflects a political world where district governance is assumed antithetical to site based or classroom operations, where management is perceived separate from teaching, where governing and leadership are at odds and where calls for the improvement of advanced, college bound secondary curricula are described in zero sum fashion from career bound and employability expectations.

Such rifts cannot continue within the professional educator or general citizen communities without the entire credibility of public education being in true danger. Consequently, what began as an effort to profile Regents curriculum and suggest where specific districts might help one another improve their subject centered, external testing formats has changed to a general argument for the survival of the Regents as a platform to stabilize all of New York public education.

Sadly, in five years, the identification of Bulls-Eye, Target and "Close" districts became less important for documenting exemplary student performances and more important in formulating a systemic reform strategy that can rebuild New York State's traditional strength in secondary education. The suggestion that Regents performance allows a language for individual districts to form a horizontal network is important to create a mediating structure to shore up public education. The Japanese concept of *kieretsu* is important to New Yorkers as a demonstration that strong competitors can create equally strong forums for collaboration.

No one knows what the 21st Century roles of the State Education Department, Governor's Office, Legislature and state level special interest groups will have become in establishing policy meanings for secondary education . Similarly, no one can project the relationships of Boards of Cooperative Educational Services, counties and city/ township municipal governments upon the daily operations of secondary education. If this text has value in influencing the politics of the near future it will be in presenting a clear and comprehensive picture of what Regents performance has meant during the first part of the 1990's decade.

Conventional responsibility and accountability for documenting secondary performance should not be ignored through variances designed to circumvent state level obligations. Taxpayers need to be informed about a vital public service and policy intentions needs to be data driven.

Neither should such reporting obligations be rationalized into obscurity as a privatized, contractual arrangement. Reporting Regents secondary program results should be continued as the precedent in New York State's public consciousness. Other measures of academic and intellectual achievement should be added to create a fuller description of school district productivity.

If technical features of presenting profiles of districts based upon State Education Department and Office of Comptroller information are controversial, then a network of high performance k-12 districts should take the predominant role in determining what information is of greatest value. This is not the time for public education to try and hide under the rock of non accountability.

Chapter One

New York's Need For *Keiretsu* in Networking Secondary Programs

Change in American public school secondary education has been described as "sound and fury signifying nothing," while the 1980's "nation at risk" reforms were purported to be "high jacked" by professional educators bent on resisting substantive change.   Actually, both charges are unfair because the turbulence of the 1980's and early 1990's did create a special era of "attention getting" politics for public educators. [1]   It is fairer to conclude that much of the ground swell about school reform for the last fifteen years has been discordant and disorganized "noise" rather than systemic "waves" of change[2] . Making sense of what has transpired demands close listening to the backbeat of educational policy and a diligent search for the nuggets of honest retrospective analysis.   For example, Joseph Murphy's general conclusion about "nation at risk" changes, written as the 1990's began,[3] is the kind of insight that cuts through the polemics about "devolution," "empowerment" and "envisioning" schools that dominated the reform movement throughout the 1980's.

> I uncovered reasons to be guarded with our claims about the likelihood of widespread fundamental reform of the American educational system....education has a tremendous capacity (and need) to deflect improvement efforts and respond to change in a ritualistic manner. Even when goodwill and commitment are widespread throughout the system, change is not a foregone conclusion. When new ideas do penetrate the system, they are more likely to be massaged to fit existing conditions than visa versa. [4]

More to the questions of organizational performance and resource distribution that   underlie this study about school district operations are Murphy's conclusions that;

> There is a fair amount of evidence that schools have a tendency to drift - or snap in some cases- back to prechange states of existance.....The connections between devolution of authority in schools and greater organizational responsiveness and effectiveness have yet to be drawn. In fact, the most thoughtful studies and reviews done to date raise serious questions about whether these outcomes are even likely.[5]

It is the institutionalization of change that focuses our attention to the meanings of persistence. Beyond the urgency of nebulous demands about a "marketplace" of choices for clients, or how to "empower" customers, rests the core institutional concern about the means to mobilize and sustain change within complex organizations.[6] The hazy and obscure nature of discussing "nation at risk" change masks two time honored debates.

First, do we think of organizations as changing through the evolutionary tendency of making piecemeal "marginal" adjustments or is the momentum of organizations exhibited in revolutionary transformations? Second, does the force of ideas carry the change agenda through the dynamics of belief and persuasion or do the structures and functions of organization channel the actions with potential for change?   The 1980's "at risk" debate fueled attempts to address such question as "either-or" confrontations and hopes for a final "all-nothing" winner.[7]

This study of the performance of New York school districts producing "college bound" secondary school graduates over a number of years assumes that the predominant view[8] about achieving persistent change is compatible to an evolutionary development of complex organizations.   Revolution is embedded within the context of institutional structures in the sense that radical change becomes "blips" of episodic unsettling. This is especially true when a public service like k-12 education has a long history of being a "domesticated" or a "near monopoly" organization with services delivered to a compulsory audience for a very long period of time.

Revolutionaries dream of the complete overhaul and full disintegration of those institutional tendencies to inch along by "successive approximations."   That dream fuels the frenzy of episodic bursts of political activity and demands that the revolution show no compromise, fear or accommodation to those who present other "contextual embedded"   arguments.   Such rigidity breeds the counterattack of like determinism from the classic evolutionist and both contribute equally to the resulting intellectual stalemate.   *Infinite regress is not the regrettable mistake but the reason for being.*   Public education in the mid 1990's does not have the luxury to prolong such a war of attrition over the equivalent of "how many angels can dance on the head of a pin" or wait out the nasty condition as combatants struggle for a "final withering away" of schooling stratification.

If change is to be legitimate, in the sense of having sustained allegiances and honest expectations for an operational future that will have enough to go around fairly, then it must stand the acid test of exhibiting itself within institutional pragmatics.   Educators must be sensitive to Murphy's conclusion about the tendency of temporarily changed arrangements to drift or snap back against the most robust revolutionary initiative.

In this sense, the fervor and performance of an embedded revolutionary effort is more analogous to the rock thrown in a pond and creating ripples outward than some transformation of water into ice or steam forms . The revolutionary might hope the turbulence created by the former will create the thinking climate for consideration of the latter (e.g., if ice meant bureaucracy regulations dissolving and steam meant thoughts about teaching-learning interactions in unique situations) *but the relationship is not automatic.* The issue of persistent change must look at the lasting impacts, if any, upon the evolutionary channels within complex organizational arrangements. In New York State and the nation, the predominant arrangements are overwhelmingly bureaucratic and corporate.

The debate about the power of ideas and beliefs upon lasting change within organizations is more difficult to answer. On the surface it seems a no-brainer. Academics huddle to do scholarly activities together. Occasionally, ideas and beliefs enter the conversations of the average university setting. The conversations center upon how ideas change things and we have the footnotes to prove it.

Yet, it is tempting to climb up on the perch of seeming neutrality-as-non involvement to discuss the channeling of policy flow as the "contemporaneous confluence of issues and choices."[9] Such descriptions seem to absolve us of the nagging questions of "speaking truth to power" and other ethical implications about the power of ideology playing as commitment to community.[10] Yet, declaring ideology as intrinsically mixed within the channeled activity of organization only shifts the debate to whether the values used to legitimize choices can be delimited to *ex post facto* rationalizations. Again, there is a *perverse* comfort in asserting that any organized decision can be rationalized as what reasonable and prudent people would do in a given situation.[11]

Yet, it seems only a small improvement to assert that the organizational nature of a "pluralistic, democratic society" makes value questions of quality, efficiency, and equity unresolvable.[12] Similarly, value loaded questions lie within the meaning of a stable or destabilized society. The concurrent description of legitimate policy as the use of operational contingency and emergency response plans in uncertain times still remains a bug-a-boo.[13]

This book is about the institution of the public school system called grade k-12 districts of New York State and the claimed legitimacy of a "college bound" production called the Regents secondary program. Within an era of widespread skepticism and growing confrontation, the 1983-1989 Regents Action Plan was declared a failure and charged with spending $3.8 billion without achieving measurable improvement in achievement results[14]

The peak of the crescendo was a Spring 1995 <u>New York Times</u> editorial calling for the abolishment of the Board of Regents. The argument was made on two grounds; the present organization of public education needed dramatic restructuring and Regents were the major impediment.[15] Legitimacy for the existing Regents institution, and the prospects for educational reform the rest of this decade, reflect New York's version of concern for organizational realignments and redirection of policies as a new mix of issues and the illusion of resolving old conflicts.[16] The study of institutional change over time suggests persistence is created by substitutions within the intrinsically unresolvable issues and fundamental tensions of American society.[17]

Consider the general confusion over the ideas of standards, goals, and outcomes that might describe expectations of a child learning. Consider the matching of sets of competencies to a particular meaning of academic production or broad classification of social intentions about "health." Are the "goals" discussed and agreed upon in the 1988 Governor's Conference in Charlottesville capable of being understood when we listen to the emotional reaction of the Right Christian speaking about "outcomes education" in the mid 1990's?

There are those who wish educational goals could be translated into measures of organizational progress presented as "vital signs."   Can vital signs proponents make sense to people who demand traditional standards capable of specifying minimal and maximum thresholds for performance to change schools?

<u>There Must Be a Way to Avoid Two Sticky Thickets</u> [18]

New York State public services cannot survive without sustaining the basic citizen perception of an institutional intention to serve the "good" of the citizens. In hard economic times or times of deep skepticism over the direction of state government, the argument about an intention of service must be buttressed with an exhibition or demonstration of such an ethic in organizational outputs.   In the mid 1980's the Reagan controlled Department of Education attempted to exhort its intentions of virtue behind the "devolving" of the federal role in education. The "bully pulpit" method of convincing the public and this form of shaping educational policy was used to excess.

In the 1990's few informed people are listening to "bully" advice because their 1980's cultivated deafness lingers on.   Survivors of the past fifteen years poften want operating demonstrations of the "good" schooling ethic operationalized in examples that can be explained directly in terms of the larger efficiency and effectiveness of the existing organization. If such descriptions are not forthcoming the citizens react angrily.

For professional educators the policy climate is worse. In spite of lofty pronouncements to promote flexibility and decentralize authority, much of the "block grant" thinking about money sent to "grassroots" organizations as "local discretion" is tied to cutting funding totals and creating a cannibal atmosphere among existing organizational educational interests.

"Gridlock, " as the first hint of getting the discussion around to production in public schools, is not an adequate description of organizational performance. The exhibits demanded by skeptical citizens are what the schools produce as bureaucratic forums and whether reform investments improve particular learning interactions. Both remain the eternal mysteries. Education appears stuck between promoting the ought and the should of a "good" school performance and conceding that an honest description of the existing arrangements complete with pragmatic references to production are not around to verify actions.

There are two forms of very sticky thickets that the advocates of New York State public education might well avoid for a period of time during the rest of the 1990's. One is the assertion of "equity" that claims there is no existing organized system currently serving 2.5 million children. What makes equity a sticky thicket is the discussion of the ideas as the universal conditions of equality; a philosophic pronouncement behind a social decree. When you are discussing equity as a form of redistributive politics within an existing institution like New York public education , the honest definition is;

> As a policy matter, equity is a complicated. It is a matter of redress rather than one of address. That is, policy makers cannot decree social equity, they can only create the laws and social programs that relieve the effects of inequity after it has been identified. The need for governmental action cannot be recognized *until some identifiable inequity has been shown to be serious and in need of a remedy. Then action is justified to the extent necessary to eliminate the identified inequity* (emphasis added)[19]

The Regents secondary "college bound" programs are not weaved back and forth as a comparative discussion of "career bound" programs (or even suggestions for policy redress) as sharing secondary curriculum until later chapters. Before then we analyze equity issues as a institutional relationship with the production of Regents secondary programs throughout the state. According to the findings here, the description of exemplary Regents performance of children is a story about the operation of sixty six generally white and wealthy suburban districts(mostly downstate around New York City). This is the predominant patterning of how student performance and the Regents curricula exhibit certain New York State k-12 districts.

The educational economist Douglas Windham argues efficiencies can be gained from lowering costs, or from better serving disadvantaged populations, or by doing both at the same time in relative proportion to one another. Each purpose leads to a different form of public service institutions acting to organizationally "be efficient" in underdeveloped countries. Windham further notes that choosing between the provision of basic and advanced schooling, servicing marginal or elite groups, and wanting massive school improvements when there are no moneys for systemic reform are common issues in underdeveloped countries.

To avoid confusion in the directions of reform, and to be able to prioritize the use of resources efficiently, there must be an explicit assertion of an intended threshold of quality as expectation of effectiveness in implementation. Professor Windham advocates for the provision of basic education to marginalized groups in underdeveloped countries as the most effective investment in promoting a country's overall productive quality.

> Study after study reveals that the children of the poor are less likely to gain access to basic education, less likely to remain after gaining access, less likely to graduate and, if they graduate, less likely to gain substantial social and economic benefits from their education. The problem rests not with the "victims" of this process; the current disillusionment often expressed by the poor toward education is fully justified given the reality of the experiences they encounter. *When society fulfills its responsibility to meet the prerequisite conditions for effective preschool, school and post school environment, these negative attitudes toward basic education will change.*(emphases added)[20]

Maybe negative attitudes about the poor will change or maybe they will not. The institutional issue of equity in policy implementation is found in how well Windham's argument for an underdeveloped country might affect the discussion of implementing equity in the present New York State public education institution.

Investing educational resources for a relatively small "college bound" elite compared to all children in k-12 schooling, can couple with generic attitudes toward education fostered by being poor in American society. American reformers [21] have argued forcefully that the inner cities (and some remote environments) in New York State are domestic versions of providing k-12 education in underdeveloped countries.

Following Professor Windham's logic within the embellishment of such a radical reformer's exhortation, the reform agenda of New York State as an equity effort seems to need an explicit assertion of the educational quality intended for "non-college bound" students. I disagree but the mastery thresholds specified must justify the institutionalized investment in Regents secondary programs as a "dependence path," a path describing basic through advanced education sequences, services delivered to elite and marginal groups and, most important, where money should be directed as school change investments in advanced secondary programs during the next twelve and twenty four months.

The second sticky thicket of dangerous misinterpretations that probably should be downplayed in discussing New York educational quality is the idea of *democracy*. The assumption about reforming schools as a particular insitutional description of what securing collaboration and commitment from a community means seems to be perpetuating intellectual *impasse'* about shared policy purposes and strategies in on-going State Education Department reform initiatives.

Professor Darling-Hammond argues that "democratic discourse" transforms a school's capacity into accepting the responsibility to decide what is "exemplary" secondary practice means. The active mind of the learner is what justifies any public institution's concern about knowing something in the first place. What goes on inside a child's head and what a teacher, parent and community member can do to facilitate intellectual and emotional connections to some form of curriculum is what all educating is about. Yet, in this case, the thicket is surely one where good intentions about preserving autonomy and authenticity also pave the road to intellectual hell by designing a political correctness straw man in the name of "removing local responsibilities."

> If the processes and outcomes of education are already defined by those outside of the schools, there is nothing left to talk about. It is the process of collective struggle that produces the vitality, the shared vision and the conviction that allows schools to redesign education in fundamentally different ways. The removal of local responsibility for thinking things through deprives schools and communities of the opportunity to engage in the kind of empowering and enlivening dialogue that motivates change. [22]

There seems no way to accommodate or mediate the following conclusions about the Regents institutional authority or Regents secondary program;

> In heavily regulated New York State, a new Compact for Learning exhorts schools to set their own goals, to engage in school based rethinking and redesign, to develop alternative assessment of student learning, to teach of understanding through interdisciplinary or inquiry based team teaching and cooperative learning, and to develop more personalized learning environments. *Yet, at the same time the curriculum is straight jacketed by Regents courses and testing requirements,* which is not interdisciplinary or inquiry based, and by directive syllabi that often maintain the view that teaching means transmitting information to be memorized within the context of the traditional age-graded, single-discipline compartments. [23]

We need to return to first premises about democratic behaviors in public institutions. Granted, the strategy of "never cooperate" is a stable equilbrium that makes it irrational for any individual to seek a more collaborative arrangement. Yet, such strategy breeds the Hobbesian solution to dilemmas of collective reform, exploitation, coercion and dependence, whether done exclusively in the name of Regents authority or local discretion.

Public education is a public service paid for by New York State citizens so that the full potential of children can contribute to the general well being of the state and the country. Even if citizens and educators continue to agree-to-disagree about a set standard of "content" or a threshold of "mastery" learning, we can all agree that New York State schools cannot find itself limiting the pool of possible children between four and twenty one years old that might be smart and talented?

The fairness criteria within "democracy" contains both the ethical obligations of a "level playing field" and the pragmatic necessity of giving every person the "benefit of the doubt" about their talent and commitment. Public education must identify the sprinkle of really talented children within the population of all those going to school. This means paying special attention to the "marginalized" groups of students that might be overlooked in an exclusively elite stratification system. But what this study will call the Bulls-Eye and Target k-12 district jurisdictions throughout the state may have few if any marginalized students. That is the sticky wicket of stratified pluralism.

Finally, when professional teachers try to improve their teaching practices or the ways teachers and administrators learn to collaborate, the honesty of "democratic discourse" is tested to the extreme. It is the exchange of ideas among intellectual peers that allows real group decision making and commitment to choices made collectively. An operating Shared Decision-Making Committee is a pragmatic illustration of a place holder mechanism. In the mid 1990's a policy analyst could honestly conclude that the structure of the State Education Department in New York State has been so undermined since 1993 that fundamental meanings of governance and accountability as state wide phenomena of institutional stability are questionable.

Is Professor Darling-Hammond correct that use of Regents curriculum and testing in itself creates an "undemocratic" climate for changing things and a "straight jacketed" school organization? In Chapter Six we will look at the use of a peculiar form of variance approval affecting some Regents curricular subjects. Variances generally allow a local school district to modify oversight expectations and create a local decision arrangement on a temporary "pilot project" basis once the state gives permission. In the last chapter we discuss the approval of counting students who score below passing (50 to 64) as meeting minimal Regents competence standards and requirements for high school graduation.

Is Curriculum Reform More Content or More Organization ?

What became clear during the "nation at risk" era was the core policy question of whether curriculum reform could be considered predominantly as a problem of content
(e.g., "frameworks") and instruction or whether the problem was more one of organization and institutionalized political context. To appreciate

the New York State story of "nation at risk" reform and one state's version of what has happened to public education during the past decade and a half, we study the Board of Regents governance and legitimizing power of the institution to justify the Regents secondary program.[24]

Classic political theory argues that ideologies guide political mobilization and actions. You must express an organized cause (usually power to the people on one side and law and order on the other) before political action resulting in change will occur. Consequently, if you want to convince people of your resolve to participate in their "at risk" situation you must have a "vision" of what they can become. They may still ignore your advice, but their attention is gained. Most of the "effective schools" arguments in the 1980's were about the image making of what could be, as opposed to the pragmatic assessments of how to translate actual curriculum strategies into organizational results.

This text is written on the alternative assumption that reform of secondary curriculum which lasts for quite a while is less about content specifics or teaching-learning interactions and more about existing institutional arrangements that provide forums for particular policy stances. For example, the confusion over the appropriate level of education government to lead and concentrate reform efforts demands a political analysis of organizational arrangements as a vertical and horizontally connected network.

In the early 1980's, the initial focus upon Regents secondary programs as a reform response was called the Regents Action Plan, essentially bureaucratic because contemporary "top down, ratchet down" implementation of the State Education Department mirrored the historic "monolithic" relationship of the Board of Regents.

My second argument for an institutional policy interpretation of curricular reform is based upon the allocation patterning and distribution scarce resources. This economic model of organization suggests that the precedent of resource allocations(e.g., annual budget) describes the institutional condition for change and adaptability.

"At risk" response is not because the frailty of a particular secondary curriculum content or testing program *per se*. Responses are based upon the patterning of "have" and "have not" jurisdictions within the overall institutionalized system called public education. If enough "have not" arrangements mobilize to create political stress for the internal organization, k-12 schooling will engage in reform spasms. Still, all complex bureaucracies "muddle through" by incremental decision making[25] so even the most urgent response seems slow.

If "extra" moneys suddenly become available (as with an "at risk" emergency response), there will be a series of lump sum add-ons to the existing allocation arrangements. This supplemental patterning assumes that the existing organization is being nourished and strengthened but not dramatically challenged as failing or replaced altogether. A strong reason both Governors Cuomo and Pataki have desired control over the

Board of Regents domain in New York State is the extent of taxpayer resources invested in the educational public service.

In 1993-1994, the state had an overall budget of nearly sixty two billion dollars (a common rumor has it that New York State expenditures are the equivalent of the 9th largest spending country in the world). The k-12 public education portion of that budget in 1993-1994 [base year of the study] was over nineteen billion dollars.

My final refection about interpreting curriculum reform in organizational terms comes from the reality of finding over arching institutional purpose within large complex institutions. The k-12 school system in New York State consists of 2.5 million public school children (and another half a million in nonpublic arrangements) going to school in 4000 buildings located in 700 school districts and part of 40 intermediate governments. The only way a system this complex makes mutual decisions or moves in a general direction is by "factoring" choices to local or subunit decision makers. [26]

It took New Yorkers seven years to appreciate this pragmatic reality in trying to reform public education. Between 1983 and 1989, state level officials assumed that commonalty could be achieved with enough curricular mandates and direct state level oversight of local practices. Complexity and fiscal crisis culminating in the early 1990's finally convinced the most die hard advocate of the "big picture" in New York State that public education could only be understood as a "grassroots" phenomenon of local actions. The policy action shifted to the k-12 district and the local building site.

During those same years many testing activities were undertaken and the results of secondary Regents course performance were summarized into official data generalities and descriptions of aggregate patterns. In effect, we can make policy sense of the Board of Regents secondary curriculum by documenting institutional patterns of actual use in local jurisdiction testing arrangements. The scope and sequence of particular Regents content, the validity of testing and the implicit production function of the Regents degree are found in the annual audit meanings of "factored" practice within the public education system of New York State. This study considers the time period between the 1987-1988 and 1993-1994 school years.

Introducing the Idea of *Kieretsu*

Public education must be strengthened in terms of the traditional legitimacy of the Board of Regents_*even while the actual structure for retaining the legitimacy should change from the conventional State Education Department domination of practice to a network of exemplary performing k-12 districts*. The Japanese argument of *Kieretsu* could be used to justify crating a strong alliance of top producing or Bulls-Eye k-12 districts. The Regents secondary program could again become the standard for academic performance identity needed to revitalize New York State education in general. Specific identification of the thirty three k-12 districts that create the best Regents secondary programs and another thirty three k-12 districts that are "close" to the exemplary standard provides a specific institutional rationale for academic performance and a target for school improvement.

The idea for encouraging systemic change in New York is that districts with strong Regents secondary programs could be the state's "best bet" for leading all educational reforms. A district with an exemplary "college bound" program and proven mastery performance over a sustained period of time should appreciate the reformer's concurrent expectation for high "career focus" standards and the obvious necessity of a strong elementary and middle school program. While the actual relationship among exemplary district remains an open question, identification of specific jurisdictions to participate within such a forum allows state level policy makers to frame concrete hypotheses about a network of operating districts that work together.

At its heart the change strategy is deliberately selective and follows the historic model of county extension agents helping farmers consider the benefits of contour plowing and corn planting in the 1930's. [27] During that time the common practice of farming was by straight line plowing. Such a method created tremendous erosion problems and very low yields in corn production. Cornell University extension agents identified farmers who would try contour plowing and let the results act as the evidence and argument given for changing other farmers minds.

Less than ten percent of all the farmers agreed to be the "innovators" in the initial experiments. Over a decade of time these demonstrators and other followers showed superior results due to the use of the new method and became, in effect, the leaders in the systemic change of the corn producing industry in New York State.

The political nature of such potential cooperation today could borrow ideas from the grouping of Japanese businesses called *keiretsu*. [28] There are two types of *kieretsu* ; <u>vertical</u> where large companies exercise decisive influence on suppliers and distribution outlets and <u>horizontal</u> where several manufacturing companies join with banks, insurance and trading companies to form an interrelated group.

Where American corporations make some effort to coordinate such vertical and horizontal interests by ownership of different stocks, the Japanese go much deeper in securing interrelationships and mutual obligations. For example, a vertical *kieretsu* of automobile making would find the parent company owning stock in the various suppliers and distributors and also teaching a common basis for quality improvement, inventory control and general management know-how. [29]

In a horizontal *kieretsu* all members of the group keep their independence, sovereignty in decision making and responsibility for outcomes in performance. The individual members even compete against one another for better performance. Although members do business within the group, no member depends on another member for more than 15 or 20 percent of its business. Top executives meet once a month for lunch and a guest speaker. No detailed business is discussed and the benefit of membership is not immediately tangible since membership does not guarantee an increase in the amount of business within the group. Instead, the equal benefit to all members is early access to information regarding business opportunities in related fields.

A horizontal *keiretsu* may decide to launch a coordinated large scale venture (e.g. the equivalent to a regional educational reform initiative). All members invest their capital, so each member's share is limited and so is the risk of loss. United as a group they can take swift and bold action. If a member company faces a crisis all the rest of the group comes to the rescue. For example, if one company has an excess of labor force, the other companies take the unneeded workers. This allows all members to have the security and stability needed to focus upon long term interests.

Obviously, the *kieretsu* concept has some strong messages of change for the American tradition of open competition and free market theory. The horizontal *keiretsu* in present day Japan (e.g.. Mitsubishi) could easily be identified to the 1880's Standard Oil monopoly of John D. Rockefeller. Yet, the ideas of such cooperation between institutional forms, blended with competition that identifies membership, seems very much suited to thinking about a persistent alliance of top Regents producing public school districts in New York State. The first step is to determine who might be in such a grouping and then refine to the core issues of making economic and educational alliances last over time.[30]

The Need for a New York Consideration

In the mid 1990's New York public education seems definitely off stride. There seems deep confusion over the implementation of the highly decentralized Compact for Learning reform agenda. Since summer of 1993 the Albany based State Education Department has twice undergone dramatic reorganization of traditionally specialized functions. Technical specialists and the bureau chief / assistant commissioner model of hierarchy relationships within the Department were both transformed. The organization was "flattened" by these middle managers being transferred or eliminated. Technicians were reassigned to generalist "field teams" and sent out across the state to "facilitate" educators in local jurisdictions. While such actions were within the sentiment of the Compact agenda as Board of Regents Goals, the result to State Education Department institutional operations was chaos. In Spring 1995, the Commissioner admitted the mistake in implementation strategy and reinstated the traditional administrative and technical functions. [he also resigned from the Commissioner position]. In the eyes of many now cynical State Education Department employees the damage to the infrastructure of regulation and oversight can not be repaired for a long time.

Second, the Republican Governor George Pataki announced an expectation of 30 percent cuts in all State Education Department programs and personnel during the Spring of 1995. More than 200 employees took advantage of early retirement options or were fired when certain program areas closed down. The political problems of reaching agreement on the state budget for Fiscal Year 1996 further exacerbated the political uncertainties in New York public education.

This state level action coupled with the federal level of government where the Republican controlled Congress froze Clinton Administration programs with recission budgets coming into New York State. The result of such delay in resource flow was especially damaging to the Albany based State Education Department personnel because sixty percent of their expected operating money comes from federal sources (e.g.. vocational education, school to work and Goals 2000).

All these changes imply a strong need for local k-12 districts to form a sustaining network alliance connected to state wide educational policy by a common concern for the Regents secondary program. These networks or areas of district collaboration are needed throughout the state. At present, most k-12 districts have associations within Board of Cooperative Educational Services areas and, despite the District Superintendent authority from the state, these are contract service arrangements within the institution.

This study of districts with exemplary Regents secondary programs assumes that there is an intense political need for grouping "lighthouse" jurisdictions in ways that BOCES regions, the present State Education Department, or even professional associations among Superintendents cannot do. New York public education must mobilize itself institutionally by creating a lattice or network structure of individual k-12 districts *regionally* that can reaffirm and sustain the traditional *state wide* power of the Regents curriculum and year end testing as an advanced secondary program.

The Rest of the Book

The following chapter will create the methodological argument for identifying thirty three k-12 districts as the Bulls-Eye or top "college bound" Regents jurisdictions in the state. Chapter Three will detail the organizational and performance characteristics that create an institutional description of the Bulls-Eye group in New York. Systematic attention will be given to the relationships of the top jurisdictions to the rest of the districts in the state. Conventional reform concerns for fiscal capability, fiscal effort and socio-economic conditions surrounding public education will guide discussion.

Chapter Four will use the idea of coming "close" to various mastery standards in Regents curriculum to identify a second group of thirty three "target" k-12 districts. This second group will be discussed as iterations of jurisdictions, both in relation to the center Bulls-Eye group and to change opportunities possible across New York State. The potential for regional networking and alliance building in geographic areas across the state will be described in terms of Regents subject performance results.

Chapter Five will briefly consider three types of special policy situations that confound full discussion of state wide secondary reform throughout New York State. Chapter Six will present optimistic implications of state wide policy based upon re-enforcing secondary Regents curriculum goals and mastery thresholds. A potential danger of using variances to blur mastery and minimum expectations for secondary performance will be noted.

---

[1] Some observers argue that the complexity of modern policy demands an issue be recognized before change can occur. In that sense, "noise" becomes important as sensitizing the possibilities of resource additions or redistribution regardless of the whether the need for change is legitimate or not. See, for example, Anthony Downs, "Up and Down With Ecology: The Attention Getting Cycle" The Public Interest, 1971 , pages. 39-50

[2] William Boyd argued persuasively that "noise" can create schizophrenic tendencies in both the actions of educators attempting reform schools and the perceptions of the American public about school change. See "Education Reform: Paranoia, Amnesia, and Schizophrenia" Educational Evaluation and Policy Studies , Summer 1987, pages 157-168

3 Joseph Murphy Restructuring Schools (New York: Teacher's College Press, 1991)

[4] ibid page 97. Also see George and Scarlett Graham, "Evaluating Drift in Policy Systems," in Phillip Gregg (ed) Problems of Theory in Policy Analysis (Lexington: Lexington Books) 1976, pages 77-87

5 Murphy, op.cit. page 95

[6] The same is true with commitments made to the "seductive nature" of teacher empowerment rhetoric. See Andrew Porter, et.al., "Reforming the Curriculum: Will Empowerment Policies Replace Control?" in Susan Fuhrman and Betty Malen(ed) The Politics of Curriculum and Testing (New York: Falmer Press), 1991. especially pages 28-29.

[7] An interesting discussion of such debate in geology is found in Stephen Jay Gould's Times' Arrow, Time's Cycle (Cambridge: Harvard University Press) 1987. In describing the "beanbag" of conflict between advocates, Gould counsels, "The arrow of homology and the cycle of analogy are not warring concepts, fighting for hegemony within an organism. They interact in tension to build the distinctions and likenesses of each creature. They interweave and hold one another, as the laws of time's cycle mold the changing substances of history. The relentless arrow of history assures us that even the strongest analogy will betray signs of uniqueness" page. 198

[8] ibid . Predominant in the sense that the "lead dog" in the sled sees differently from other members in the team. As point-counterpoint discussion Gould notes, "Any taxonomist will tell you that they must, above all, separate analogous from homologous similaries, discard analogies and base classification on homologies alone. But any functional morphologist will pass over homologies as simple repetitions and seek analogies that teach us about the limits of variety when separate lineages evolve structures for similar functions." page. 198

9 Suzanne Estler, "Decision Making" in Boyan(ed) Handbook of Research in Educational Administration, (New York: Longmans) 1988, Chapter Fifteen

10 when the guide word is ethnic there is no more wiggle room. See Daniel Patrick Moynihan's Pandaemonium (New York: Oxford University Press) 1993

11 ibid. " Order in an Age of Chaos" pages 143-174. Also see Graham Allison's argument that this condition is found as the instrumental rationality of foreign policy. See Essence of Decision , (Boston: Brown, Little) 1971. Irving Janis, Sanctions for Evil , (San Francisco: Jossey Bass), 1978, sees such technical perversity as the "groupthink" behavior of small groups under extreme stress.

12 Robert Stout, et. al., "The 'What' of the Politics of Education" in Jay Scribner and Donald Layton (ed) The Study of Educational Politics (New York: Falmer) 1995, page 16.

13 Moynihan op cit. "Ethnicity as a Discipline" pages 27-62. It is interesting to compare how similar the concerns about institutions and the value of stability in the 1960's are with today's worries of competitiveness and achievement. See Donald Schon Beyond the Stable State (New York: Random House) 1967

14 For the initial analysis when events were happening see the Business Council of New York, Where did the Money Go? (Author: Albany, 1988) For an excellent overview of the same policy question several years later see Hamilton Lankford and James Wyckoff, "Where Has the Money Gone? An Analysis of School District Spending" Educational Evaluation and Policy Analysis (Summer 1995) pages 195-218

15 The New York Times, April 15, 1995, Editorial Page.

[16] Laurence Iannaccone and Frank Lutz, " The Crucible of Democracy: The Local Arena" in Jay Scribner and Donald Layton (ed) The Study of Educational Politics (New York: Falmer Press, 1995) pages 39-52

[17] ibid See discussion of the "urban" rationale for focus of the vast majority of policy concerns about public education. page 50

[18] my apologies to cricket fans in Britian and other Commonwealth countries that know the difference between wicket used in sport and inferences about the conceptual jungle of excessive American adhesions described here.

[19] W. Garms, et. al, School Finance: The Economy and Politics of Education (Englewood Cliffs: Prentice Hall), 3rd Edition, 1989 page 92.

20 Douglas Windham, " The Role of Basic Education in Promoting Development: Aggregate Effects and Marginalized Populations" Advances in Educational Productivity, 2, 1992, page 92

[21] For example, Jonathan Kozol Savage Inequalities (New York: Longmans) 1992

[22] Linda Darling Hammond " Revitalizing Educational Reform" Phi Delta Kappan , June 1993, page 761

[23] ibid page 755

[24] In case New York State educators are exhausted by the intensity of legitimization battles see the Italian situation in Robert Putnam's " Changing the Rules: Two Decades of Institutional Development, " Making Democracy Work (Princeton: University Press, 1993) pages 17-60.

[25] Charles Lindblom" The Science of Muddling Through" Public Administration Review, 1959. Also see Charles Averech, et. al. Do Schools Make a Difference? (Santa Monica: RAND) 1971 and Milbrey McLaughlin, "The RAND Change Agent Study Revisited" Educational Researcher, 1991

[26] Putnam op cit "Social Capital and Institutional Success" pages 163-180

[27] Charles Lionberger, The Process of Change (Ames: University of Iowa Press) 1962

[28] Kosaku Yoshida, "New Economic Principles in America- Competion and Cooperation" California Management Review , Fall 1990, pages 2-14

[29] William Powell, "Neither Market Nor Hierarchy" Review of Organizational Behavior, 1990, pages 293-336.

30 J. Weiss and Andre Delbecq, 'High Technology Cultures and Management: Silicon Valley and Route 128" Group and Organizational Studies, March 1987, pages 1-12

Chapter Two

Rules for Modeling Curriculum Production

New York is a very complex state, with more than 2.5 million school aged pupils organized in more than 700 school districts. Individual jurisdictions range from New York City with 950,000 students to several k-12 districts with student bodies of less than 100. The first methodological task for making sense of educational expectations translated into indicators is to describe parameters that allow a credible meaning of a *state wide policy system*. The parameters of the system tell the reader what is being described and, just as important, what is deliberately excluded from the study. Anyone who attempts this task knows from the outset that the results will be controversial.

This illustration of a statewide system in New York State limits the description to school district jurisdictions with a full grade k-12 structure and focuses upon results from the college bound Regents secondary curriculum program. It further confines the time period for study to the seven years between the 1987-1988 and 1993-1994 academic years. The special condition of the City of New York district and three secondary only districts are discussed separately. Public school jurisdictions with less than a full grade k-12 complement are not included.

The result of such deliberate delimitation shape the interpretation of educational policy results within the district meaning of an operating state wide system. The 649 New York State k-12 school districts used in this analysis are a somewhat different "cut" from the conventional State Education Department practice of including all districts with eight or more full time equivalent (FTE) teaching staff. The 649 jurisdictions with a full k-12 grade structure make more sense for a study of secondary programs than the 694 districts that FTE teachers generate.[1] While studying the increases in real expenditures in districts centers upon teacher compensations and spending for disabled pupils[2] several large elementary and middle school districts in the New York City metropolitan area skew the institutional properties supporting secondary curricula efforts that guide this study.

It was important to specify productivity outcomes capable of being understood nationally and by the State of New York in a direct and particularistic manner.   Although nationally norm standardized test results are highly popular, the Regents Diploma and Regents secondary course work represent the deepest historic sense of institutional investment, especially in a particular scope and sequence of secondary school curriculum. That long standing meaning of scope and sequence is both subject focused as an assumption of extracting from performance standards and external tested performance of secondary grade students as assessment standards extensions.[3]

New York State has been engaged in two very different curriculum reform agendas, each generating new distinctions between separate arenas for the policy discussions about performance, content, teaching and assessment during the seven year period of this study.

This study argues systematic analysis must begin and end with an the priori description of the policy environment one hopes to inquire about. The description of the original stage set is a pragmatic outline of study intentions. Many times the parameters selected for framing a "do-able" study will not be what the researcher would argue as an optimum or maximum preference.   To establish a basis for generating research questions about an operating policy system, for example, the analyst must choose between a preliminary task of studying the rationale behind the spectrum of organizationally defined graduation expectations or simply assert the Regents diploma is the premier "college bound" degree given.

Such an assertion does not blind the researcher to Regents alternatives(see Chapter Six discussion) but does mean that diploma and graduation credential alternatives to the Regents degree are implied as either delimited or exceptional cases. Backward mapping of such patterns of "paradoxical" relationships helps identify the full spectrum of public educating. If a district was identified with more than 90 percent of seniors intending to go on to college yet Regents diplomas were given to less than 10 percent of graduates this would establish a logically paradox condition.

If the Regents degree were the *only* premier credential within New York State then there should be only one set of districts with the best college bound secondary programs. If exceptions are found by looking at descriptive information of particular districts, they are evaluated as either incidental "outliers" or as a documentation of alternative non-Regents degree in "college bound" patternings within the state.

A second example of conceding pragmatic limit is the use of official Office of the Comptroller information with State Education Department to identify a general set of indicators influencing statewide system productivity. The State Education Department uses in-process estimates of revenues and expenditure patterns. The Office of Comptroller gives final and audited figures. The researcher trade-off is being current, since the Comptroller municipal report is a one year delay. In addition, the New York State Legislature required the annual "condition of education" report be prepared for the citizens of the state by the State Education Department on the Board of Regents behalf.

The pragmatic question for systematic analysis of statewide educational policy questions is whether a state wide study of secondary program results can be done so that the reader gains important institutional and systemic insights while remaining sensitive to the lack of methodological purity.

The Process of Systematic Interpretation

The study of New York State public education, as a deliberately defined institution operating a state wide policy system, cannot pretend to the classic methodology of empiricism. Instead of assumptions about the research "laboratory" environment capable of controls and manipulation, policy analysis must make due with intellectually framing the found situation. The logic behind systematic interpretation of an embedded condition describes a multiple step process of approaching the given information as an already existing yet ever changing data set. Even the conventional identifications of dependent and independent variables in a statement of researchable relationships must be liberally modified into associations of connected or "clusters" of logic patterning. The steps described to be taken concern the operation of secondary programs in New York State k-12 jurisdictions. Each step translates to policy as an expression of the selection bias and specific decision rule preferences used by the researcher .

Step One established Regents Diploma performance as the primary production focus of this study and, as such, a major indice of outcome for the statewide system. The initial analysis of 649 k-12 districts applied a three-fifths or 60 percent Regents Diploma graduation rate as a demonstration of "high" productivity between 1987-1988 and 1993-1994 academic years.

Step Two identified a second subgroup of districts where seniors registered an intention to be "college bound" after high school graduation. New York districts were identified by expectations by 85 percent or slightly more than four fifths of the seniors indicating "college bound" intentions between 1987-1988 and 1993-1994 school years.

Step Three first established mastery standards for performance in nine Regents courses for the three years between 1991-1992 and 1993-1994 . Specific decision rules were created for each of the nine courses according to the percentage of students taking the year end examination and the percentage of those students that successfully pass the examination.

• The standard of 80 percent taking the year end test and 80 percent of those students successfully passing the test was established for Global Studies, History and Government, Biology and Intermediate Mathematics.

•The standard of 67 percent taking the year end test and 80 percent of those students successfully passing was established for Chemistry and Advanced Mathematics.

•The standard of 40 percent taking the year end test and 80 percent of those students successfully passing was established for Physics, French and Spanish foreign languages.

All 649 k-12 districts in the statewide population were classified in terms of zero to nine possible "advanced points" for one year of the Regents subjects, then aggregated for the three years under study.

Step Four identified a final subgroup of districts that were "close" to the Regents Diploma or Regents subject course work standards. A "close" district had an exemplary indicator in either taking the year end test or passing the subject but not the right proportion. Because any decision rule to establish the threshold of production is suspect as an arbitrary cut-off point there must be a concession to the idea that districts that are "close" to the standard of excellence need to be also identified.

Step Five described the overlapping subgroups of districts identified in previous steps as they formed a "pool" of New York districts with exemplary Regents academic productivity outputs.   This subset of all New York State districts were prioritized by point counts and described in terms of a number of indices (i.e., k-12 enrollment, pupils per square mile, dollars spent per child in average daily membership, combined wealth ratio of the district, the percent of children using free or reduced lunch subsidy, the annual teacher turnover, the percent of secondary school dropout).

The Originally Modeled State wide System.

The 649 New York k-12 jurisdictions can be described by official education statistics as the statewide system and then compared to both the general statistics of the state and the particular statistics for the district of New York City.

Table 1-1 shows how this analysis differs in substantive ways from the official New York: State of Learning profile which includes the City district. The influence of New York City in both meanings of the state wide system of 718 districts and as a single district of nearly one million children standing alone is obvious. In key socio-economic indices, the inclusion of New York City and less than k-12 grade districts substantially changes the percents of free and reduced lunch participation from just under 30 percent to slightly under half the children in the state (48.8 percent).

One statistic that has no ready explanation is the "college bound" percentage of 80 percent reported by the official state profile New York: State of Learning and the slightly more than 76 percent reported by my analysis.

Table 1-1
649 District Model Compared to Official 1993-1994 Data
About State k-12 System

	Statewide Model Used Here			New York : State of Learning	
ndicator	Min	Average	Max	State	New York City
#Districts		649		718	1
#Counties		57		6	5 boroughs
Regents Diplomas	0	42.9%	100	38%	21%
College Bound	7.2	76.4%	100	80.3%	81.9%
Enrollment	64	2,547	46,248	3 ,637	971,690
Pupil/Sq Mile	0.33	153.2	856.0	1 89.9	3000+
$CAADM	$5,401	$8,532	$35,382	$8,241	$7,495
CombWealthRatio	0.21	0.97	9.26	0.99	0.97
Free Lunch	0	29.6%	100	48.8%	79.2
Tch Turnover	0	7.2%	29.0	8%	13%
Dropout	0	2.0%	9.7	4.0%	6.2%

An important aspect of this study was to describe the state wide system of k-12 districts over a long enough period of time that trends and persistent characteristics could be identified. The seven year period presented in Table 1-2 contained two distinct reform agendas, the latter part of the 1980's Regents Action Plan and the 1990's beginnings of the Compact for Learning initiative.

While the ebbs and flows of academic performance are based upon many influences, it seems fair to infer the state wide efforts at systemic reform did reshape New York State secondary education.

Table 1-2
649 Districts Modeled Between 1987-88 and 1993-94 School Years

Indicator	1988	1989	1990	1991	1992	1993	1994
Regents Diplomas	51.2	38.5	40.6	40.2	40.9	41.8	42.9
College Bound %	66.1	68.4	70.1	71.9	74.7	75.4	76.4
Enrollment	2415	2412	2417	2452	2472	2515	2547
Pupil/Sq Mile	150.1	150.1	150.2	151.1	151.3	151.2	153.3
$CAADM	**	6619	6519	6846	8415	8492	8532
CombWealthRatio	.95	. 95	.95	.95	.98	.97	97
Free Lunch%	no rept	no rept	20.0	20.5	22.1	29.6	29.6
Tch Turnover%	9.7	9.7	9.3	8.7	9.6	7.3	7.2
Dropout%	3.0	3.1	3.0	2.6	2.4	3.2	2.0

** in 1988 per pupil spending reported by district enrollment, not average daily membership

Using the seven year time frame to establish a benchmark of average district performance, we find the 1993-1994 academic year provides an *equivalent* measure for Regents Diplomas produced (42.2 percent) but is *greater* in college bound expectations, (71.1percent) money spent per child, ($7542 average) and free and reduced lunch use (24.9 percent). The 1993-1994 year average is *less* than the seven year average in teacher turnover (8.9 percent) and secondary dropout (2.7 percent).

Grouping by the 60 Percent Regents Diploma Output

In Table 1-3 we can see that, with the exception of the 1987-1988 school year, the Regents degree productivity of the state has been around two fifths of the graduating seniors. As a first step in establishing an "advanced curriculum" argument about productivity those districts with more than three fifths or 60 percent of graduating seniors receiving a Regents diploma for academic years 1987-1988 through 1993-1994 were identified.

It is apparent that 1987-1988, the year prior to full implementation of the Regents Action Plan reform agenda (New York's response to "nation at risk"), is very different from the next six years in Regents diploma productivity. In 1987-1988 a fourth(26%) of all k-12 districts in the state graduated three fifths of their seniors with Regents diplomas. The next year, 1988-1989 only four percent of k-12 districts in the state reached the 60 percent level. Throughout the early 1990's approximately five percent of New York's districts have exceeded the three fifths percentage threshold.

Table 1-3
Districts With More than 60 Percent Regents Diploma Graduates

Indicator	1988	1989	1990	1991	1992	1993	1994
#Districts	172	27	36	32	28	42	62
#Counties	47	17	23	16	13	20	24
Regents Diploma as % of statewide pop.	26%	4%	5%	5%	4%	6%	9%
College Bound %	71.1	76.0	79.8	83.9	86.2	85.9	86.1
Enrollment	2641	1791	2459	2788	2692	2 803	2532
Pupil/Sq Mile	138.9	118.0	107.5	241.1	181.9	144.0	194.1
$CAADM	**	7,182	6,963	7,922	10,140	10,701	9,644
CombWealthRatio	1.03	1.36	1.24	1.51	1.61	1.73	1.30
Free Lunch%	no rept	no rept	12.8	7.7	8.8	11.2	14.9
Tch Turnover %	9.0	10.9	9.3	8.5	9.3	7.7	7.5
Dropout%	2.8	2.0	2.0	1.4	1.3	2.9	1.0

When 1993-1994 academic year is compared to the seven year span as an average it is clear that the low Regents producing years between 1988-1989 and 1991-1992 raise the question of whether a trend of steady improvement is a fair conclusion. Those educators and citizens who appreciate persistent and systemic change as a long term effort are happy to see that more than sixty districts or nine percent of all New York jurisdictions are "high" Regents degree producers in 1993-1994.

For those who perceive the glass half full, 1993-1994 could be interpreted as the slow revival of public education credibility after three years of plateau; college bound expectations holding steady at four out of five seniors, twenty more districts than the previous year reporting more than three fifths' percentage their graduates with Regents diplomas. In addition, both teacher turnover and secondary dropout show a sharp reduction from the turn of the decade.

What is most interesting about the related inference of "college bound" expectations of graduating seniors is the suggestion that the percentage of Regents graduates dropped dramatically in 1987-1988 , but the expectations of seniors to be "college bound" continued to rise for all seven years into the mid 1990's.

Compared to the general population of 649 k-12 districts in the statewide system, the districts producing more than three fifths of their graduates with Regents diplomas are distinctive in spending per child, the combined wealth of the local community and fewer pupils using free and reduced lunch programs. The pupil per square mile measure seems to indicate that the 1990-1991 and the 1993-1994 academic years contained a different, more densely populated set of qualifying districts.

Embedding Regents Diploma Outcomes With College Bound Intentions

The indicator of college bound expectations would seem to logically embed actual Regent degree productivity. As a first cut, the three fifths)Regents degree producing districts were cross-referenced to the those with college bound expectation exceeding 85 percent.

Table 1-4 illustrates that *adding the eighty five percent college bound expectation to the 60 percent Regents degree productivity does refine the sub population of exemplary districts considerably.* More important for the argument of an expanded production measure, there is a better argument that the Regents degree and the intentions about college bound were becoming more coherent as the seven year period progressed.

Table 1-4
Districts With 60% Regents Diploma Graduates and 85+% College Bound

Indicator	1988	1989	1990	1991	1992	1993	1994
#Districts	27	11	14	20	18	29	40
#Counties	12	7	9	7	7	13	15
Regents Dip%	70.3	66.8	66.8	66.0	67.6	64.5	65.4
College Bound	89.4	91.6	91.3	91.6	92.1	92.1	92.3
Enrollment	2851	2119	3396	3322	2627	3358	3154
Pupil/Sq Mile	260.4	2 13.4	221.8	198.6	353.0	231.4	288.3
$CAADM	**	9246	8015	9035	10450	10266	10575
CombWlthRatio	1.81	2.16	1.68	1.95	1.86	1.67	1.57
Free Lunch %	no rept	no rept	2.9	3.7	7.1	8.2	3.4
Tch Turnover	9.2	9.8	8.7	8.7	9.9	7.7	7.6
Dropout	2.7	0.7	0.9	1.0	2.8	0.9	0.9

The 60/85 production group of districts will be discussed as Bulls-Eye jurisdictions throughout the rest of the text. During the seven year period, the elite districts were considerably larger and more dense than the state average. Yet, there is an indication of internal variation or that the same districts were not in the 60/85 classification each year. When the average enrollment and pupil per square mile indices are compared for 1992, 1993 and 1994 there is an indication that the actual districts reaching the mastery production threshold are different enough for further inquiry.

"bedrooms" communities for commuters. Many of these districts have developed secondary curriculums that are competitive with state level Regents efforts to create "advanced" courses. In such a case, a district may deliberately not emphasize the Regents credential and substitute their "local" diploma instead. *Certain districts claim that public education offered locally is superior to any state level standards, including the Regents curriculum and degree.*

Consequently, certain districts claim that they are very strongly oriented to "college bound" expectations, but that their curriculum and diploma of choice are *not* within the Regents program. Although New York City was not included in this analysis as a statewide system of 649 jurisdictions , it should be noted that the City district with its 950,000 pupils would fit with this particular subgroup classification. In 1992, when New York City produced only 19.7% Regents diploma graduates, 84.5% of senior students indicated an intention to be college bound.

Figure 1-1 lists those eleven k-12 districts that averaged less than one in ten(10%) of their graduates receiving a Regents diploma but more than 90 percent of their seniors indicating college bound intentions for 1991-1992 , 1992-1993 or 1993-1994 academic years.

Figure 1-1
90+ Percent College Bound in Non Regents Degree Districts

			1991-1992		1992-1993		1993-1994
Distrinct	County	Regents	Col Bound	Regents	Col Bound	Regents	Col Bound
Brighton	Monroe	8.2	92.8	4.1	93.8	3.2	94.1
Herricks	Nassau	1.1	97.0	1.7	100.0	4.9	93.2
Southold	Suffolk	X	X	X	X	1.2	92.2
Bryam Hills	Westchester	0	96.0	0	97.3	0	97.6
Blind Broook	Westchester	0	98.3	0	97.6	0	91.8
Chappaqua	Westchester	1.9	95.6	1.0	91.3	0	96.5
Mamaroneck	Westchester	0	89.9	0	86.0	0	95.6
Bronxville	Westchester	0	97.0	0	87.9	0	100.0
Edgemont	Westchester	0	98.2	0	98.1	0	95.3
Irvington	Westchester	0	96.4	0	93.6	0	92.3
Scarsdale	Westchester	0	97.5	0	99.7	0	94.3

x =Southold exceeded the minimum Regents threshold

Selecting The Top Regents Degree Producing Districts

The combination of Regents degree production and extremely high college bound expectations of graduating seniors do not automatically coincide. While consideration of individual Regents coursework provides a persuasive picture of some exemplary secondary program efforts, there is no parallel reporting of equivalent local or non Regents course work. Because of the inherent ambiguity, the description of k-12 districts making the best efforts in secondary programs is also a study of decision rule impact as the Regents program is emphasized.

Table 1-5 presents the sixty six New York State districts that would meet the criteria for the first decision rule; 60 percent Regents degree production and 85 percent "college bound" intentions in at least one year between 1987-1988 and 1993-1994. We can see that two districts, Jericho in Nassau County and Westhill in Onondaga County, maximized the decision rule by exceeding the threshold for each of the seven years. We can also see that the numbers of districts meeting the first decision rule varied by individual year.

Actual application of this rule generated two groups of jurisdictions; districts meeting the decision rule criteria for one or more years and other jurisdictions that were "close" to the threshold. A "close" district violated the a priori 60/85 *proportion* rule for Regents degree and college bound production. For example, a "close" jurisdiction might graduate 58 percent Regents students, but have 90 percent college bound intentions.

Table 1-5 also illustrates the internal ebb and flow of Regents degree production between the 1987-1988 and 1993-94 school years. This period maps the time of changeover from Regents Action Plan to Compact for Learning reform agendas. One might suggest that the shift from "top down, ratchet down" reform to "bottoms up, grassroots" reform initiatives had a direct impact upon districts providing Regents secondary programs. Regents proponents would be happy to note the gradual but steady improvement in numbers of New York districts meeting such a high productivity standard.

Identifying where the best Regents degree production takes place seems to mean secondary programs in the suburbs near four of New York's five largest cities. The only surprise is the lack of qualifying districts around Buffalo (Erie county).

Table 1-5
Seven Year (1987-1988 to 1993-1994) Production Analysis
New York Districts Graduating 60% Regents Diplomas and 85% College Bound

		Year Graduating							
	County	1988	1989	1990	1991	1992	1993	1994	Total
North Colonie	Albany				X	X	X	X	4
Voorheesville	Albany					X			1
Alfred Almond	Alleghany							X	1
Chenango Forks	Broome						X		1
Maine-Endwell	Broome		X		X			X	3
Vestal	Broome	X					X		2
Spackenkill	Dutchess							X	1
Williamsville	Erie	X			X				2
Amherst	Erie						X		1
Newcomb	Essex		X						1
Long Lake	Hamilton	X							1
Herkimer	Herkimer	X							1
Geneseo	Livingston							X	1
Honeoye Falls	Monroe			X			X		2
Penfield	Monroe						X		1
Pittsford	Monroe	X		X	X	X	X	X	6
W. Irondequoit	Monroe							X	1

Table 1-5 Continued

	County	1988	1989	1990	1991	1992	1993	1994	Total
Bellmore-Merrick	Nassau							X	1
East Willistone	Nassau							X	1
Garden City	Nassau	X		X	X	X	X	X	6
Hewlett-Woodme	Nassau						X		1
Jericho	Nassau	X	X	X	X	X	X	X	7
Locust Valley	Nassau	X						X	2
Lynbrook	Nassau	X			X				2
Massapeaqua	Nassau				X				1
Manhasset	Nassau				X		X	X	3
Plainview	Nassau						X	X	2
Rockville Ctr	Nassau	X	X	X	X	X		X	6
Roslyn	Nassau	X			X	X	X	X	4
Syosset	Nassau				X		X	X	3
Wantagh	Nassau							X	1
New Hartford	Oneida		X	X	X		X	X	5
Jamesville-DeWitt	Onondaga	X		X	X	X			4
Fayetteville	Onondaga	X		X	X	X	X	X	6
Skaneateles	Onondaga					X	X		2
Tully	Onondaga							X	1
Westhill	Onondaga	X	X	X	X	X	X	X	7
Cornwall	Orange							X	1
Monroe-Woodbur	Orange			X					1
Cooperstown	Ostego		X						1
Mahopac	Putnam							X	1
Clarkstown	Rockland		X						1
Nanuet	Rockland					X	X		2
S. Orangetown	Rockland		X				X		2
Shenendehowa	Saratoga							X	1
Cold Spring Harb	Suffolk	X	X	X		X	X	X	6
Commack	Suffolk							X	1
Elwood	Suffolk					X	X	X	3
Half Hollow Hills	Suffolk		X	X	X	X	X	X	6
Harborfields	Suffolk	X							1
Kings Park	Suffolk	X							1
Miller Place	Suffolk	X						X	2
Mt. Sinai	Suffolk							X	1
Pt. Jefferson	Suffolk						X	X	2
Shelter Island	Suffolk	X	X		X				3
Sayville	Suffolk				X				1
Smithtown	Suffolk						X		1
Southold	Suffolk							X	1
Three Village	Suffolk	X		X			X	X	4
West Islip	Suffolk							X	1
Gananda	Wayne						X		1
Ardsley	Westchest	X					X	X	3
Briarcliff Man	Westchest	X	X			X	X		4
Hastings/Hud	Westchest		X					X	2
Pelham	Westchest				X				1
Pleasantville	Westchest		X	X	X			X	1
		22	15	14	21	16	28	39	

The New York City metropolitan counties of Nassau, Suffolk, Rockland and Westchester provide thirty seven of the sixty six (56%) jurisdictions that met the 60/85 standard in at least one year. Among the fifteen very top producers, those who reached the 60/85 threshold at least four of the seven years, there are nine districts in the New York City area(60 %) and three districts from Onondaga county surrounding Syracuse.

"Close" Districts as Regents Production Outcomes

Appendix A identifies seventy eight k-12 districts in the state who were "close" to the 60/85 threshold for graduate production in 1991-1992, 1992-1993 or 1993-1994. As noted earlier, "close" is often an issue of proportion. Bethlehem district in Albany county, for example, barely missed the decision rule threshold in 1991-1992 with an 59/83 ratio and in 1992-1993 with a 60/84 ratio. Under the "close" calculation of 1/2 point per year, Bethlehem earned one "advanced" curriculum point for performances in those two years.

In all, 144 of 649 New York State k-12 districts received at least one 1/2 "close" point for Regents Degree production.   The general argument could be made that 20 percent or one in five New York districts have a strong tendency toward high college bound expectations and high Regents degree production.   Clinton district in Oneida county, Liverpool in Onondaga county, Niskayuna in Schenectady county, Northport and Westhampton Beach in Suffolk county were "close" to the 60/85 threshold for all three years.

Figure 1-2 summarizes the production point totals for districts exceeding the 60/85 diploma threshold for 1987-1988 through 1993-1994 combined with "close" pointd added to that standard during the 1991-1992 through 1993-1994 period.

Figure 1-2
Districts With 60% Regents Diplomas and 85% College Bound Standards,
and "Close" Points Added (1992-1994)

District	County	Total	#Dists
Jericho	Nassau	7	
Westhill	Onondaga	7	
Rockville Center	Nassau	6 1/2	
Garden City	Nassau	6	
Fayetteville-Manilus	Onondaga	6	
Pittsford	Onondaga	6	
Cold Spring Harbor	Suffolk	6	
Half Hollow Hills	Suffolk	6	
New Hartford	Oneida	5 1/2	
			9
Briarcliff Manor	Westchester	4 1/2	
North Colonie	Albany	4	
Roslyn	Nassau	4	
Jamesville-DeWitt	Onondaga	4	
Three Village	Suffolk	4	
Pleasantville	Westchester	4	
Maine-Endwell	Broome	3 1/2	
Manhasset	Nassau	3	
Syosset	Nassau	3	
Elwood	Suffolk	3	
Shelter Island	Suffolk	3	
Hasting on Hudson	Westchester	3	

District	County	Figure 1-2 Continued Total	# Dists
Williamsville	Erie	2 1/2	
Locust Valley	Nassau	2 1/2	
Voorheesville	Albany	2	
Vestal	Broome	2	
Plainview	Nassau	2	
Honeoye Falls-Lima	Monroe	2	
Skaneateles	Onondaga	2	
Tully	Onondaga	2	
Nanuet	Rockland	2	
S. Orangetown	Rockland	2	
Commack	Suffolk	2	
Harborfields	Suffolk	2	
Miller Place	Suffolk	2	
Port Jefferson	Suffolk	2	
Sayville	Suffolk	2	
Smithtown	Suffolk	2	
Southold	Suffolk	2	
			17

Looking at Specific Regents Courses in the Secondary Curriculum

In the educational indicator discussion to this point, the concept of standards was considered as a productivity measure of degrees upon graduation. Standards set as a threshold of advanced performance at the outset is one thing, standards established to differentiate patterns within an existing system of operation quite another. This goes to the core of the paradox when "authentic assessment" is discussed abstractly as a learner centered expectation of high performance, and then discussed as "portfolio evidence" that can compare students for ranking.

When we start with policy interest in the existing Regents course curriculum of New York State, the concept of mastery standards can only be created as "decision rules" of specific requirements of mastery in on-going practice. Such rules can be created on any basis, and its pragmatic credibility depends upon discussing the underlying rationale for each particular rule. The following scheme for classifying "mastery" in Regents course work is based upon a number of specific assumptions governed by the official information provided by the State Education Department.

First, the official information giving the number of pupils successfully passing a Regents year end exam when expressed as a percentage of average grade enrollment centers the policy question on the present program structure of a district.

The second assumption about the official information provided is *through a combination of percent taking the year end test and percent successfully passing the examination.*

The combination is assumed to create a more appropriate two tiered measure of actual performance that percent sucessfully passing the year end examination.

Third, that district performance in Regents curriculum should be assessed on a multiple year basis. In this analysis, the performance of districts are evaluated for the 1991-1992, 1992-1993 and 1993-1994 school years.

Fourth, nine of twelve possible Regents curriculums reported by k-12 districts to the state were assessed, but Beginning Math, English and Earth Science courses deliberately not included in this study of courses. The reason for excluding the three courses is due to the growing practice of using these courses for non college bound and non advanced curriculum students. As we will discuss in the last chapter, the use of another peculiar variance expands the number of suspect Regents courses. Circumventing conventional curricular evaluations of mastery and minimal thresholds have been evident in Regents Beginning Math , Comprehensive English and Earth Science courses for some time. From an organizational perspective of scheduling the secondary curriculum there is nothing intrinsically wrong with this practice but it does confuse the policy orientation toward mastery in advanced or "college bound" evaluations.

Fifth, for this study there are three different sets of "mastery thresholds" established to evaluate the results of secondary pupil performance. A district could achieve up to nine advanced secondary curriculum credits for each year (analysis was done for three years) if academic performance exceeds the stipulated thresholds established for different courses. Specifically:,

• Four Regents courses would be differentiated as college bound and a district would achieve an advanced secondary curriculum credit point for each course *if four fifths of the students enrolled in the course actually took the year end examination and, of those, a minimum of four fifths successfully passed the examination.* The 80%/80% decision rule would apply to the Regents courses in Biology, Global Studies, History /Government and Intermediate Mathematics (Math 2).

•Two Regents courses would be identified as "general advanced" and a district would receive an advanced credit point for each course *if two thirds of the students enrolled in such a course took the year end examination and, of those, four fifths successfully passed the examination.* The 67%/80% decision rule would apply to the Regents Chemistry and Advanced Mathematics (Math 3) courses.

•Three Regents courses would be identified as "elective advanced" courses. A district would receive an advanced credit point for each cours*e if two fifths of the enrolled students took the year end test and of those four fifths successfully passed the exam.* The 40%/80% decision rule would apply to the Regents Physics, Spanish and French courses.

Table 1-6 summarizes the districts that have exceeded the mastery threshold for at least five Regents courses during those years.
[other "close" districts are identified in Appendices B through J]

Table 1-6

Districts Exceeding Mastery Thresholds in Five or More Regents Subjects, 1991-1994

District	County	Glb	Hist	Fren	Span	M2	M3	Biol	Chem	Phy	Total
					1991-1992						
Garden City	Nassau	X	X	NO	X	X	X	X	X	X	8
East Willistone	Nassau	X	X	NO	X	X	X	X	X	NO	7
Cold Sp. Harbor	Suffolk	X	NO	X	NO	X	X	X	X	X	7
Minerva	Essex	X	X	X	NO	NO	X	X	X	NO	6
Great Neck	Nassau	X	NO	NO	X	X	NO	X	X	X	6
Jericho	Nassau	X	NO	NO	X	X	X	X	X	NO	6
Roslyn	Nassau	X	X	NO	X	NO	X	X	X	NO	6
Westhill	Onondaga	X	X	NO	X	X	X	X	NO	NO	6
Syosset	Suffolk	X	X	NO	X	X	NO	X	NO	X	6
Herricks	Nassau	X	X	NO	X	X	NO	NO	X	NO	5
Rockville Center	Nassau	X	NO	NO	X	NO	X	X	NO	X	5
Jamesville-Dewitt	Onondaga	NO	X	NO	X	X	NO	X	X	X	5
Wayne	Wayne	X	X	NO	NO	X	X	X	NO	NO	5
Ardsley	Westchester	X	NO	NO	X	X	NO	X	NO	X	5
Garden City	Nassau	X	X	NO	X	X	X	X	X	X	8
Syosset	Nassau	X	X	NO	X	NO	X	X	X	X	7
Rockville Center	Nassau	X	X	NO	X	NO	X	X	X	X	7
Jericho	Nassau	X	X	NO	X	X	X	X	X	NO	7
Fayetteville-Manl	Onondaga	X	X	NO	NO	X	X	X	X	X	7

District	County	Glb	Hist	Fren	Span	M2	M3	Bio	Che	Phy	Total
					1992-1993						
Cold Sp. Harbor	Suffolk	X	X	X	NO	NO	X	X	X	X	7
Windham-Ashl	Greene	X	X	X	X	NO	X	X	NO	NO	6
East Willistone	Nassau	X	X	NO	X	NO	X	NO	X	X	6
Herricks	Nassau	NO	N	NO	X	NO	X	X	X	X	6
Clarkstown	Rockland	X	X	NO	X	X	NO	NO	X	X	6
Mt. Sinai	Suffolk	X	X	NO	X	X	NO	X	X	NO	6
Briarcliff Manor	Westchester	NO	NO	X	X	NO	X	X	X	X	6
Amherst	Erie	X	X	NO	NO	X	X	X	NO	NO	5
Keene	Essex	X	NO	X	NO	X	NO	X	NO	X	5
W. Irondequoit	Monroe	X	NO	NO	X	X	NO	X	X	NO	5
Roslyn	Nassau	NO	X	NO	X	NO	X	NO	X	X	5
Clinton	Oneida	X	X	NO	X	X	NO	X	NO	NO	5
Westhill	Onondaga	X	X	X	NO	X	NO	X	NO	NO	5
Three Villages	Suffolk	X	NO	NO	X	X	X	NO	NO	X	5
Half Holllow Hills	Suffolk	X	NO	NO	X	NO	X	X	X	NO	5
Commack	Suffolk	X	X	NO	X	X	NO	X	NO	NO	5
Wayne	Wayne	X	X	NO	NO	X	X	X	NO	NO	5
Rye	Westchester	NO	X	NO	X	NO	X	X	X	NO	5

Table 1-6 Continued

District	County	Glb	Hist	Fren	Span	M2	M3	Bio	Che	Phy	Tot
East Willistone	Nassau	X	X	NO	X	X	X	X	X	X	8
Syosset	Nassau	X	X	NO	X	X	X	X	X	X	8
Jericho	Nassau	X	X	NO	X	X	X	X	X	NO	7
Garden City	Nassau	X	X	NO	X	X	NO	X	X	X	7
Half Holl ow Hills	Suffolk	X	X	NO	X	X	NO	X	X	X	7
Amherst	Erie	X	X	X	X	X	NO	X	NO	NO	6
Pittsford	Monroe	X	NO	NO	X	X	X	X	X	NO	6
Herricks	Nassau	X	NO	NO	X	X	NO	X	X	X	6
Great Neck	Nassau	X	NO	NO	X	NO	X	X	X	X	6
Rockville Center	Nassau	X	NO	NO	X	NO	X	X	X	X	6
Roslyn	Nassau	X	NO	NO	X	X	X	NO	X	X	6
Clinton	Oneida	X	X	NO	X	NO	X	X	X	NO	6
Fayettville-Manlius	Onondaga	X	NO	NO	NO	X	X	X	X	X	6
Skaneateles	Onondaga	X	X	NO	NO	X	X	X	X	NO	6
Elwood	Suffolk	X	NO	NO	X	X	X	X	X	NO	6
Kings Park	Suffolk	X	NO	NO	X	X	X	NO	X	X	6
Byram Hills	Westchester	X	NO	NO	X	X	X	X	X	NO	6
Briarcliff Manor	Westchester	NO	X	NO	X	X	NO	X	X	X	6
North Colonie	Albany	X	X	NO	NO	X	X	X	NO	NO	5
Weedsport	Cayuga	X	X	X	NO	X	NO	X	NO	NO	5
Manhasset	Nassau	X	NO	NO	X	X	NO	X	NO	X	5
Cold Sp. Harbor	Suffolk	X	X	X	NO	NO	NO	NO	X	X	5
Miller Place	Suffolk	X	X	NO	X	X	X	NO	NO	NO	5
Mt. Sinai	Suffolk	X	X	NO	X	X	X	NO	NO	NO	5
Port Jefferson	Suffolk	NO	X	NO	X	NO	X	X	NO	X	5
Ardsley	Westchester	NO	X	NO	NO	NO	X	X	X	X	5
Pelham	Westchester	X	X	NO	X	NO	NO	X	NO	X	5

The case for metropolitan "down state" being the location of the most advanced Regents course credit districts is inferred when we delimit this assessment to the top ten Regents course work performers between 1991 through 1994.   Only Fayetteville-Manlius, near Syracuse, is listed but not in the metropolitan New York City area.

There is quite an encouraging sign of Regents improvement when we consider the numbers of districts exceeding a total of five points accumulation during the three years of analysis. Fourteen districts in 1991-1992 expand to twenty three districts the folowing year and twenty seven districts in 1993-1994.

Combining "Advanced" Coursework With "Advanced" Degree Production

It would seem reasonable to expect that high percents of Regents diplomas received would match with districts with high numbers of mastery threshold points for Regents course work.

Yet, Table 1-7 demonstrates we must approach our desired objective step by step as the *crucial unit of analysis* shift from the district as a mechanism of productivity (and structuring jurisdiction) to sets of courses throughout the secondary grades.

Table 1-7
Final Classification Combining Courses and Regent Diploma Points

District	County	Courses	Diploma	Final
Total				
Garden City	Nassau	23	6	29
Jericho	Nassau	20	7	27
Cold Springs Harbor	Suffolk	19	6	25
Rockville Center	Nassau	18	6	24
Syosset	Suffolk	21	3	24
Fayetteville-Manlius	Onondaga	17	6	23
East Willistone	Nassau	21	1	22
Roslyn	Nassau	17	4	21
Westhill	Onondaga	11	7	18
Briarcliff Manor	Westchester	14	4	18
Half Hollow Hills	Suffolk	12	6	18
Manhasset	Nassau	14	3	17
Herricks	Nassau	17	0	17
Ardsley	Westchester	10	3	13
Amherst	Erie	11	1	12
Mt. Sinai	Suffolk	11	1	12
Pittsford	Monroe	6	6	12
Clinton	Oneida	11	0	11
Great Neck	Nassau	11	0	11
Wayne	Wayne	10	0	10
Elwood	Suffolk	6	3	9
Jamesville-DeWitt	Onondaga	5	4	9
Three Village	Suffolk	5	4	9
North Colonie	Albany	5	4	9
Skateateles	Onondaga	6	2	8
Kings Park	Suffolk	6	1	7
Miller Place	Suffolk	5	2	7
Port Jefferson	Suffolk	5	2	7
Bryam Hills	Westchester	6	0	6
West Irondequoit	Monroe	5	1	6
Pelham	Westchester	5	0	5
New Hartford	Oneida	0	5	5
Pleasantville	Westchester	0	4	4

Foremost, the Regents diploma demands both a minimum number of secondary subject credits (18.5), but also particular scope and sequencing of Regents or advanced placement courses. As noted earlier in the initial discussion of Regents diplomas in New York State, receipt of the credential has fluctuated with the statewide reform agenda during the past decade.

This look at a statewide k-12 system of k-12 organization, described with several indicators of curricular production, is a far cry from some dreams of finding "authentic outcomes of learning and achieving standards." It does make a strong case, however, that the core methodological issue of evaluating systemic change within compulsory institutions is more than a simple acknowledgement of input and conversion indices related to output measures.

Aggregate graduation rates in all forms of curriculum programs(including Regents) must be systematically analyzed with a particular scope and particular sequencing of courses taken in mind. Identifying the relationship of curriculum outcomes to actual groups of involved pupils is the obvious next methodological issue to focus directly upon issues of organizational aggregation.

The thirty three k-12 districts identified in Table 1-7 form the Bulls-Eye for those targeting the best in Regents college bound productivity in New York State.   It is important to note that Herricks, Clinton, Great Neck, Wayne and Pelham districts made the final list of exemplary Regents performers *despite missing the Regents diploma production threshold for all seven years.*   Herricks district in Nassau county is one of the eleven districts in the state where more than 90 percent of seniors expect to go to college, but less than 10 percent receive a Regents diploma.

Figure 1-3 extends the Table 1-7 profile by showing the county concentrations of the very best Regents diploma and course work production. These are suburban k-12 districts in four of New York's fifty seven counties:

Figure 1-3
Counties Where the Bulls-Eye Districts Are Concentrated

Nassau County	Onondaga County	Suffolk County	Westchester
East Williston	Fayetteville-Manilius	Cold Spring Harbor	Ardsley
Garden City	Jamesville-DeWitt	Elwood	Briarcliff Manor
Great Neck	Skateateles	Half Hollow Hills	Bryam Hills
Herricks	Westhill	Kings Park	Pelham
Jericho		Miller Place	Pleasantville
Manhasset		Mt. Sinai	
Roslyn		Port Jefferson	
Rockville Center		Three Village	
Syosset			

Rather than apologize for finding a jurisdiction issuing their own local graduation diplomas while operating a secondary program exemplary enough to make the top billing, the sensitivity of the model to detect such anomaly cases should be a comfort to state level policy makers in New York State.

Tentative Results Inferred From Steps of Systematic Interpretation

The New York State story of advanced secondary programs in k-12 public school districts leads to several conclusions about on-going practice. However, before drawing inferences we must remind ourselves that there were several crucial delimitations to this particular study. Districts with less than a full k-12 grade complement (including three senior high school districts) and the supersize New York City district were not included in the study.   In short, the meaning of state wide population modeled for this particular description was 649 jurisdictions out of a possible 718 districts in the state.

Second, combining the generalized expression of intent to the particular rates of Regents diploma graduation necessitated a stringent +60 percent diploma &+85 percent "college bound" expectation threshold to justify a cohesive pool of districts. In other words, Regents diploma output as a dependent variable of district productivity cannot be considered to automatically reflect a more generalized expectation of going to college among all New York high school seniors. Indeed, one of the districts in the final pool of top producing Regents college bound jurisdictions graduates less than 10 percent of seniors with the Regents diploma.

Third, to establish any trend of organizational patterns there must be at least three years data collection. For tracing aggregate diploma "output" in any state as turbulent and complex as New York during the "nation at risk" reform years a minimum of seven years seems reasonable.

Finally, the identification of 33 exemplary k-12 districts that meet the various mastery threshold criteria, and pools of other jurisdictions that were "close" to the different standards, provide the critical target identity necessary to frame further policy questions about resource distribution and wealth capabilities of k-12 organizations. We now have a vehicle to determine equivalent systems of district performance in Regents secondary activities. New York State, as a model of 649 public school districts operating between 1987-1988 and 1993-1994 , can compare specific meanings of curricular productivity to features of institutional investment.

While educational policy makers in New York State are exhorted to consider the widely publicized value of implementing national academic standards, or to discuss international competitors, there is comfort in describing the internal policy lessons of Regents production and what they can tell us about establishing "mastery" threshold identities. Such information is most useful when New Yorkers want to talk about a common basis for reforming high quality secondary education.

---

[1] Hamilton Langford and James Wyckoff, "Where Has the Money Gone?" Educational Evaluation and Policy Analysis Summer 1995, footnote nine, page 216

[2] ibid. Langford and Wyckoff claim New York school districts spent $12 billion more on public k-12 education in 1991-1992 than in 1979-1980. School districts increased real expenditures per pupil by 46% over the 1980-1992 period

[3] I am skating dangerously close to the late 1980's national standards controversy. If what Christopher Cross argues is the pragmatic reality of that controversial topic, then New York State's "last state holdout" as a subject centered and external tested secondary program should be reinforced as a guard against against the whirlpool tug. Mister Cross states:
The current standards debate is a tangled and indecipherable web to the public and probably most educators. Most projects focus on performance standards , but some are concerned with teaching standards, and others with assessment. It has been difficult to establish a common vocabulary. One of my modest proposals would be to ban the word "standards" unless it is preceded by the proper modifier so that everyone can understand what kinds of standards are being discussed.
Developing performance, content, teaching and assessment standards are separate and distinct activities. Performance standards define what a student should know and be able to do, whereas

content standards describe the material to be taught to ensure that students can meet performance standards.   Teaching standards outline the skills and competencies that teachers need to provide learning opportunities and experiences for students to be able to master performance standards.   Assessment standards identify the essential criteria for determining whether students have met the specified performance standards. (emphases added) page 45. See "Implications of Subject-Matter Standards" in Nina Cobb (ed) The Future of Education: Perspectives on National Standards in America (New York: The College Board) 1994

Chapter Three

Bulls-Eye Districts and Horizontal Networking

Following the mastery threshold argument presented in the previous chapter, thirty three k-12 districts were selected from a pool of 649 k-12 jurisdictions as having the best Regents college bound programs in the state. If the overall target for curricular improvement is the Regents college bound focus, then the thirty three districts are the "Bulls-Eye" of the present New York State situation.

Districts accumulated productivity "mastery points" for exceeding an "output" standard of 60 percent Regents diploma graduates and at least 85 percent of seniors indicating college bound intentions. If a district exceeded the graduation threshold for each of seven years under analysis, that jurisdiction would achieve 7 mastery points.

Districts accumulated course work points for exceeding a mastery threshold in nine specific Regents subjects. If a district exceeded the mastery threshold in all nine subjects for each of three years under analysis, that jurisdiction would achieve 27 mastery points.

Districts that were "close" to the productivity expectation in nine Regents subjects , but missed the proportion standard, could accumulate 1/2 point per year between 1990-1991 and 1993-1994 school years.

In sum, the thirty three New York State districts with the best Regents secondary programs were identified as the Bulls-Eye group. These jurisdictions that achieved between 4 and 29 points based upon the mastery standards. Garden City and Jericho districts in Nassau county received the highest number of mastery points among the thirty three Bulls-Eye jurisdictions. New Hartford district in Oneida county, Pelham and Pleasantville districts in Westchester county received the lowest number of points to still be included in the best district grouping.

Comparing Best Districts With the Rest of the State

Table 2-1 demonstrates how special the character of the final thirty three Regents college bound districts is when compared to the averages of the 649 districts in the statewide model, the averages of the Regents graduation only group of 60+/85+ percentage districts and the group of non Regents but exemplary (-10/90+) districts identified in the previous chapter.

Table 2-1
Comparing the Bullseye Group to Other Group Identifications, 1993-94

Indices	Statewide 1993/94 Avg	Graduation Only 60/85 Avg	Non-Regents Best -10/90+ Avg	Min	Final Bulls-Eye Districts Avg	Max
# Districts	649	40	11		33	
# Counties	57	15	4		9	
Regents Diploma	42.9	65.4	0.8	4.9	60.3	75.2
College Bound	76.4	92.3	95.8	81.2	92..8	100.0
Enrollment	2547	3154	2196	107	2936	7069
pup/sq. mile	153.2	288.3	410.4	21.9	293.9	1012.0
$ CAADM	8,532	10,575	12,421	6.842	11,083	17,590
Comb Wlth Ratio	0.9	1.57	2.49	0.62	1.79	3.71
Free Lunch %	29.	7.8	1.8	0.0	6.0	20
Tch turnover%	7.2	7.7	8.0	4.0	7.4	10
Dropout %	2.0	0.9	0.5	0.5	0.8	2.2

While useful in distinguishing between the various sub groupings that formed during the process of consideration (.i.e., while making the final choice of the top Regents college bound districts) the reader should remember that some individual districts are counted in several classifications. For example, Pelham, Bryam Hills, Wayne, Great Neck, Clinton and Herricks districts received no "diploma" points for 60/85 graduation. The twenty seven other Bulls-Eye jurisdictions would also be calculated with the 60+/85+ group.

A Closer Look at the Organization

Table 2-2 presents an organization and sociological characteristic of the Bulls-Eye Regents college bound districts in New York. The ethnicity of the student body was identified as both the percentage of white students and percentage of "other" category.

In New York State reporting, the "other" classification would likely contain Asians and/or Native Americans. Only Herricks, Syosset and Ardsley districts have "other" category students exceeding ten percent.   It is   quite clear that   the districts with the top Regents secondary programs in New York State have a distinct lack of Afro American and Hispanic students enrolled. Eight of the top Regents districts had virtually all white (+95%) student bodies.

Table 2-2
Organization Characteristics of Final Bulls Eye Districts

District	93-94 Enroll	Buildings in District #Elem	#Mid	#Sr. Hi	Racial/Ethnic % White	%Other
North Colonie	5073	6	1	1	91.9	-
Amherst	2784	2	1	1	88.8	-
Pittsford	5154	2	1	1	87.8	-
West Irondequoit	3842	6	2	1	92.7	-
East Willistone	1432	1	1	1	89.5	-
Garden City	3044	4	1	1	93.5	-
Great Neck	5462	4	2	2	81.2	10.0
Herricks	3487	3	1	1	70.0	26.0
Jericho	2105	2	1	1	87.9	-
Manhasset	2258	2	0	1	79.6	10.0
Rockville Center	3220	5	1	1	83.1	-
Roslyn	2489	3	1	1	81.1	9.0
Syosset	5277	7	2	1	85.3	13.1
Clinton	1780	1	1	1	97.4	-
New Hartford	2961	3	1	1	96.0	-
Fayetteville-Manilus	3967	3	2	1	94.4	-
Jamesville-DeWitt	2402	3	1	1	87.4	5.1
Skaneateles	1732	2	1	1	99.2	-
Westhill	1871	2	1	1	95.9	-
Cold Spring Harbor	1480	1	1	1	97.7	-
Elwood	1923	2	1	1	81.7	5.6
Half Hollow Hills	7069	6	2	2	79.8	7.4
Miller Place	2665	2	1	1	90.8	
Mt. Sinai	2077	1	1	1	95.6	-
Kings Park	3142	2	1	1	95.5	
Port Jefferson	1097	1	1	1	90.7	-
Three Village	6777	5	2	1	90.7	5.5
Wayne	2692	3	1	1	97.3	-
Ardsley	1657	1	1	1	79.2	15.4
Briarcliff Manor	1071	1	0	1	91.1	7.4
Bryam Hills	1879	2	1	1	93.4	4.3
Pelham	1759	4	1	1	84.6	5.6
Pleasantville	1289	2	0	1	90.9	5.4

The largest district in the statewide model of 649 jurisdictions, the City of Buffalo district with 46,000 pupils, has nine high schools. The demographics of the thirty three top Regents program districts indicated only two districts, Great Neck and Half Hollow Hills, have two high schools.   Half Hollow Hills, Three Village, Great Neck, Syosset, Pittsford and North Colonie exceed 5,000 pupils in grades k-12. At the other end of the organizational scale, four districts had less than 1500 pupils in grades k-12.

<u>Costing Out The Top Secondary Programs</u>

Because the educational meaning of high quality performance centers upon k-12 jurisdictions, the idea of best secondary programs implies more an organizational focus than a purely academic consideration.   In other words, it is legitimate to consider the policy meanings of program achievements as the channels of organization that house educational production.   With the identification of districts with the best Regents curriculum productivity as a function of graduation rates and performance in courses we can infer a profile of how such jurisdictions operate. [1]

Table 2-3 presents four indices of general wealth capability often used in fiscal analyses of public school jurisdictions. The full valuation per child is the actual value of taxable real property on the tax rolls (determined by applying the final regular equalization rate established by the State Board of Equalization and Assessment for the rolls used to levy taxes for school purposes) for the 1993 fiscal year divided by the number of children enrolled in the district.

The Census Poverty Index number for a district is determined by the State Education Department officials as they calculate disaggregation of the 1990 Census for the county to individual school jurisdictions. The lower the number, the richer the district according to Census calculation of socio-economic information.

The percentage of free and reduced lunches is determined by the local school administrator who verifies a standard of family poverty level. The combined wealth ratio is used distributing state aid and is of calculated by real property and local sales tax paid by citizens of the district.

It is obvious that the there are some very rich districts in the Bulls-Eye group.   The Nassau county districts of Great Neck, Garden City, Manhasset, Jericho and Roslyn and the Port Jefferson district in Suffolk county all exceed $1,000,000 in full valuation of real property per enrolled child for fiscal year 1993.   Cold Spring Harbor in Suffolk county and Bryam Hills in Westchester county exceed $900,000 in full valuation per child.

A closer look at what taxpayers pay for the high quality college bound Regents programs in New York shows the 1990's decade identified by rapidly rising property values for local jurisdictions and concurrent efforts by local boards of education to keep the tax rate per $1000 assessed valuation down.

Table 2-3
Bulls Eye Districts to General Wealth Capability Indices, 1993

District	County	FullValuaton perChild,93	Census 1993	Free Lunch	Comb Wealth
NorthColonie*	Albany	480,000	3	8	1.28
Amherst	Erie	368,000	4	20	1.60
WestIrondequoit	Monroe	295,000	2	6	1.23
Pittsford	Monroe	379,000	1	4	1.63
EastWilliston	Nassau	894,000	4	1	2.51
GreatNeck	Nassau	1,367,000	3	10	3.50
GardenCity	Nassau	1,047,000	2	0	2.77
Herricks	Nassau	667,000	2	2	1.71
Manhasset	Nassau	1,230,000	2	5	3.71
Jericho	Nassau	1,383,000	2	1	3.41
RockvilleCenter	Nassau	571,000	2	2	1.90
Roslyn	Nassau	1,097,000	1	8	3.04
Syosset	Nassau	889,000	3	17	0.80
NewHartford	Oneida	301,000	6	7	1.02
Jamesville-Dewitt	Onondaga	418,000	4	12	1.36
Westhill	Onondaga	219,000	2	5	0.85
Fayetteville-Manl.	Onondaga	294,000	2	4	1.36
Skaneateles	Onondaga	298,000	4	11	1.05
ColdSpringHarbor	Suffolk	933,000	1	5	2.93
Elwood	Suffolk	555,000	3	7	1.19
HalfHollowHills	Suffolk	832,000	3	8	1.51
MillerPlace	Suffolk	315,000	3	9	0.71
Mt.Sinai	Suffolk	285,000	3	6	0.62
KingsPark	Suffolk	477,000	3	5	1.14
PortJefferson	Suffolk	1,209,000	8	12	2.18
ThreeVillage	Suffolk	421,000	2	6	0.88
Wayne	Wayne	240,000	5	17	0.82
Ardsley	Westchester	584,000	2	5	1.77
BryamHills	Westchester	968,000	2	1	2.72
BriarcliffManor	Westchester	741,000	1	1	2.65
Pelham	Westchester	838,000	4	0	2.02
Pleasantville	Westchester	565,000	2	0	2.12

* = districts are arranged in order of official New York State School Code

The Bulls-Eye grouping are especially sensitive to the impact of local economics. On average, state aid revenues make up only a fifth of all money received by Bulls-Eye jurisdictions. Table 2-4 extends the analysis of full valuation per pupil by listing both the 1990 values (rounded to nearest 000) and the percentage of change between the 1990 and 1993 fiscal years. Four of the group had real property assessments rise more than ten percent each year for the four year period.

The tax rate per $1000 is the tax levy included in the school budget adopted in the spring for the upcoming school year. The full amount of this levy is received by the district, since counties are required to cover all deliquencies.[2] As expected with the rapid rise in full valuation assessments, the tax rate per $1000 has shown a steady drop throughout the 1990's. By the end of fiscal year 1993, no Bulls-Eye district was above $19.00 per $1000. It is interesting to note those districts that are reducing their tax rate per $1000 faster than the full valuation per pupil is increasing.

Table 2-4
Bulls Eye Districts to Wealth Effort & Tax Rate Indices

District	County	FV/Enrl (000) 90	%Chg F V 1993-90	Tax Rate 1990	Tax Rate 1993	% Chg Rate
North Colonie	Albany	307	36.0	13.51	10.40	-29.9
Amherst	Erie	261	29.1	20.29	17.93	-13.2
West Irondequoit	Monroe	251	14.9	17.63	17.44	- 1.1
Pittsford	Monroe	315	16.9	16.75	17.26	+ 3.0
Garden City	Nassau	636	39.3	14.01	10.11	-38.6
Rockville Center	Nassau	463	18.9	19.30	16.84	-14.6
East Williston	Nassau	739	17.3	15.64	13.49	-15.9
Roslyn	Nassau	825	24.8	14.82	12.78	-16.0
Manhasset	Nassau	968	21.3	14.15	11.69	-21.0
Great Neck	Nassau	1046	23.5	13.58	11.34	-19.8
Herricks	Nassau	522	21.7	16.74	14.72	-13.7
Syosset	Nassau	686	22.8	13.59	12.00	-13.3
Jericho	Nassau	1110	19.7	12.4	-11.00	-12.8
Clinton	Oneida	149	27.0	19.27	16.02	-20.3
New Hartford	Oneida	218	27.6	18.11	16.39	-10.5
Jamesville-Dewitt	Onondaga	304	27.3	18.91	15.10	-25.2
Westhill	Onondaga	197	10.0	16.56	18.14	+8.7
Fayetteville-Manlius	Onondaga	2226	23.1	19.45	18.66	- 4.2
Skaneateles	Onondaga	222	25.4	18.29	15.11	21.0
Three Village	Suffolk	238	43.5	23.16	15.57	-48.7
Port Jefferson	Suffolk	475	60.7	21.54	13.81	-56.0
Mt. Sinai	Suffolk	209	26.7	19.53	17.34	-12.6
Miller Place	Suffolk	177	43.8	20.65	14.34	-44.0
Elwood	Suffolk	414	25.4	16.57	14.44	-14.8
Cold Spring Harbor	Suffolk	788	15.5	13.18	11.12	-18.5
Half Hollow Hills	Suffolk	627	24.6	13.94	12.08	-15.4
Kings Park	Suffolk	390	18.2	17.71	16.15	- 9.7
Wayne	Wayne	205	14.6	14.64	14.93	+ 1.9
Ardsley	Westchester	429	26.5	22.12	16.94	-30.6
Pleasantville	Westchester	383	32.2	21.36	15.21	-40.4
Bryam Hills	Westchester	614	36.6	14.96	10.89	-37.7
Briarcliff Manor	Westchester	457	38.3	19.42	13.61	-42.7
Pelham	Westchester	481	42.6	20.60	13.08	-57.6

The policy analyst considers such fiscal information as the first stepping stone to appreciating why changes might be occurring in particular districts. Three such explanations could be a dramatic change in the numbers of enrolled students, an alteration of the portion of revenues coming from other than local sources or that the ratio of overall revenues to overall expenditures are affected by special debt service expenditures.[3]

When a district invests in new technology or builds an addition to some structure the expenditures may temporarily exceed revenues by a great amount, creating a proportionate imbalance. For this study, all ratios of spending to revenues or total expenditures to specific functions like teaching or administrative have been done with debt service costs removed.

Table 2-5 presents data on the 1989-1990 k-12 enrollment and percent of changes in enrollment between 1989-1990 and 1993-1994 school years (The reader may wish to refer back to Table 2-2 to see the 1993-1994 enrollment figures). Similarly, the percent of state aid received by each district , the change in state aid percents between 1991-1992 and 1992-1993 and the 1993 ratio of total revenues to expenditures per district minus principal and interest debt service payments are given.

Table 2-5
Bulls Eye Districts to Possible Fiscal Explanations

District	County	Enrl 1990	%Chg Enrl 1994-90	% St.Aid 1993	%Chg St.Aid 1992-93-	Diff Rev P&I,
North Colonie	Albany	4644	+8.5	21.6	-1.0	95.8
Amherst	Erie	2625	+5.7	16.6	-0.02	97.5
West Irondequoit	Monroe	3348	+12.9	24.3	+2.1	96.0
Pittsford	Monroe	4891	+5.1	16.9	+0.06	96.1
Garden City	Nassau	2875	+5.6	6.4	-0.02	97.0
Rockville Center	Nassau	3101	+3.7	10.1	-0.05	98.3
East Williston	Nassau	1243	+13.2	7.4	+0.06	95.3
Roslyn	Nassau	2429	+2.4	5.7	-1.1	98.7
Manhasset	Nassau	2103	+6.9	6.8	-2.2	92.3
Great Neck	Nassau	5313	+2.7	5.8	-0.04	97.3
Herricks	Nassau	3260	+6.5	11.4	-1.8	94.5
Syosset	Nassau	5178	+1.9	8.5	-0.04	99.3
Jericho	Nassau	1911	+9.2	5.8	-0.02	98.5
Clinton	Oneida	1569	+11.9	48.1	-1.1	83.8
New Hartford	Oneida	2923	+1.3	29.8	-1.5	94.9
Jamesville-Dewitt	Onondaga	2169	+9.7	28.8	-1.5	95.1
Westhill	Onondaga	1528	+18.8	39.2	-1.0	94.6
Fayetteville-Manlius	Onondaga	3775	+4.8	19.0	-0.00	97.3
Skaneateles	Onondaga	1646	+5.0	29.0	-0.05	92.5
Three Villages	Suffolk	6976	-2.9	32.9	-1.3	97.1
Port Jefferson	Suffolk	1673	-52.5	8.9	-0.04	96.3
Mt. Sinai	Suffolk	1628	+21.6	46.7	-0.06	87.7
Miller Place	Suffolk	2651	+0.5	42.4	-1.0	95.8
Elwood	Suffolk	1944	-1.1	25.2	+0.09	98.5
Cold Spring Harbor	Suffolk	1254	+15.3	7.4	-0.07	98.7
Half Hollow Hills	Suffolk	7448	-5.4	14.7	+0.07	97.9
Kings Park	Suffolk	3255	-3.6	27.9	+0.07	97.2
Wayne	Wayne	2417	+10.2	44.2	+3.9	89.9
Ardsley	Westchester	1445	+12.8	8.8	-0.04	96.1
Pleasantville	Westchester	1092	+15.3	10.4	-3.2	98.1
Bryam Hills	Westchester	1639	+12.8	6.8	-0.03	95.6
Briarcliff Manor	Westchester	979	+ 8.6	7.7	-1.5	98.2
Pelham	Westchester	1618	+8.0	10.6	+0.09	95.7

The reason for the fiscal situation at Port Jefferson district becomes immediately apparent when we see that the enrollment has dropped more than 50 percent and what was a jurisdiction enrolling 1600+ children in 1990 has become slightly less than 1100 children in four years. The enrollment drop, coupled with receiving less than ten percent of revenues from the state, contributes to *the dramatic increase in full valuation per enrolled pupil and reductions in tax rates per $1000* citizens are forced to pay shown in the previous table.

For the ratio of revenues to expenditures all districts in the Bulls-Eye group generated more revenues than what they spent, once debt service were extracted. For example, North Colonie district in Albany county with a ratio of .958 had a total revenue for 1993 of $35, 427,000, a total expenditure of $36, 237,000 and an expenditure without debt service of $34,700,000. The impact of debt service payments is shown in the case of Clinton district in Oneida county. This jurisdiction had 1993 revenues of $11,900,000, total expenditures of $11,931,000 but expenditures with debt service removed of $9,999,000 to generate a ratio of .838.

The general fiscal profile of the Bulls-Eye group suggests a final perspective of the money spent to deliver high quality secondary programs to select New York children and several internal patterns of spending. While the data presented in this chapter has been compiled from the Office of Comptroller annual reports on the fiscal year of the state[4] the New York State Education Department presents a indice on expenditures per pupil unit. The indice, called Combined Aid per child in Average Daily Membership (hereafter $CAADM) includes all expenditures charged to general, debt service and special aid funds.[5]

As an organizational measure, the $CAADM shows the aggregate changes in spending throughout the district where the secondary program occurs. Table 2-6 presents the $CAADM per pupil measure for the 1993-1994 school year and the percent of change in the $CAADM for each district since the 1989-1990 year. It seems clear that certain districts with large $CAADM in 1993-1994 (+$10,000) have been increasing spending per child rapidly (Port Jefferson, Mount Sinai) while others have not (e.g., Herricks, Cold Spring Harbor). On the other hand, the district with the lowest $CAADM, Clinton district in Oneida county, increased $CAADM nearly 25 percent in five years.

Table 2-6 also presents information calculated on the basis of Comptroller data. *The reader should be cautious that the Office of the Comptroller and the State Education Department use different definitions of expenditure indices.*

The Comptroller definition of the "teaching" spending is "expenditures related to instruction in a teaching-learning situation where the teacher is regularly in communication in a systematic program. Included in this indice are salaries of teachers, teacher's aides, secretaries, clerks, teaching equipment, tuition, books and other contractual expenditures for regular and special schools."[6]

The general support indice gives a measure of district wide administrative costs, described by the Comptroller as including spending for " board of education, district clerk, chief school officer, tax collection, legal, central data processing,special items such as judgment claims and other support services."[7]

Table 2-6
Bulls Eye Districts to Spending Per Child, on Teaching and General Support

District	County	$CAADM 1993-94	%Chg 90-94 $CAADM	%Tch 1993	%Chg 92-93 Teaching	%Gen Supp 1993
North Colonie	Albany	7193	24.6	58.5	+2.5	4.0
Amherst	Erie	9588	27.3	47.8	-5.0	4.9
West Irondequoit	Monroe	8221	23.6	58.3	+1.2	6.3
Pittsford	Monroe	8822	22.1	64.9	+3.1	3.4
Garden City	Nassau	11956	17.3	60.4	+1.4	4.8
Rockville Center	Nassau	1087	19.9	57.1	-0.0	5.2
East Williston	Nassau	13648	15.3	54.3	+10.7	6.1
Roslyn	Nassau	14187	22.3	51.2	-2.6	5.1
Manhasset	Nassau	15522	26.5	59.7	-1.8	5.4
Great Neck	Nassau	1628	21.2	57.1	+1.3	4.7
Herricks	Nassau	11776	15.6	58.9	+0.0	4.6
Syosset	Nassau	11611	19.7	58.6	+3.6	4.9
Jericho	Nassau	15843	23.6	50.9	+0.2	5.8
Clinton	Oneida	6842	24.4	64.3	+5.4	7.7
New Hartford	Oneida	7665	19.4	60.3	-1.9	6.5
Jamesville-Dewitt	Onondaga	9250	19.1	46.7	-14.5	3.3
Westhill	Onondaga	7161	26.6	55.5	+5.5	4.5
Fayetteville-Manlius	Onondaga	7181	21.4	61.0	-0.0	4.6
Skaneateles	Onondaga	7484	23.2	59.9	+1.9	6.2
Three Village	Suffolk	10468	22.6	59.5	0.05	5.4
Port Jefferson	Suffolk	17590	42.9	58.4	-2.8	5.6
Mt. Sinai	Suffolk	10929	40.2	58.7	+0.05	6.9
Miller Place	Suffolk	8395	24.1	67.8	+0.05	5.7
Elwood	Suffolk	11702	19.6	59.9	+0.09	6.1
Cold Spring Harb	Suffolk	12467	13.0	56.0	+0.05	6.0
Half Hollow Hills	Suffolk	11991	22.4	60.5	-1.7	3.2
Kings Park	Suffolk	11451	19.2	60.4	-1.4	4.5
Wayne	Wayne	8272	28.9	43.7	-4.1	4.6
Ardsley	Westchester	12095	21.2	52.5	-0.02	8.6
Pleasantville	Westchester	11038	15.4	58.9	+4.1	7.0
Bryam Hills	Westchester	11677	15.1	57.5	+8.1	5.2
Briarcliff Manor	Westchester	13345	22.0	57.6	-0.03	7.1
Pelham	Westchester	13222	22.3	48.0	10.2	4.2

<u>Putting It Together</u>

The idea of *keiretsu* in organizational arrangements is a common bonding among industries with a strong need for alliance. Vertical arrangements involving sharing control with suppliers on one side and distributors on the other is easy for educators to understand. When professionals within a public school district have strong, positive relationships with both the general community (e.g. parents, board of education members) and specific organizations for secondary school graduates to continue productive lives (e.g. employment in industry, access to postsecondary schoolirg) the district has the potential of sustaining a vertical form of *keiretsu*.

Yet, the concept of horizontial *keiretsu* needs more thought for appreciating a potential public school application. Here the investors in organizations share a common sentiment that the individual competition among districts needs to be within a collective forum. If the thirty three districts that have been identified as the Bulls-Eye group center a change effort based upon horizontial *keiretsu* sentiment, there would have to be evidence and a persistent justification of a common identity. The present reward and recognition system within New York State education does not automatically provide such a sentiment.

There are, of course, various educational organizations that exist to help coordinate these districts in some fashion. Similarly, most of the jurisdictions are located in the New York City metropolitan area, some would share BOCES intermediate government contacts. Because most of the Bulls-Eye districts are rich and they may share memberships on interest groups designed to protect the fiscal advantages of "have" jurisdictions. [8] Finally, the different professional and citizen groups associated with the governance of educational matters form general alliances(e.g. superintendents, school boards, teachers) to discuss common problems.

The premise of this study is that the validity of obtaining mastery points for identification as a Bulls-Eye district with an exemplary secondary Regents program can be extended into a rationale for a network of such organizations with a horizontial *keiretsu* sentiment. The rationale for a close knit identity among the thirty three districts depends upon whether the high and low point getters in Regents performance share enough common organizational character that they can think in terms of mutual interests and change strategies as a Bulls-Eye group.

But a Bulls-Eye identity would not be automatic. There are, after all, individual districts that would have to be convinced of a need for shared actions. Herricks and Bryam Hills districts deliberately graduate less than ten percent of their seniors with Regents diplomas. The argument that high achievement in Regents courses would, by itself, create a sentiment to promote a mutual strategy for "college bound Regents programs" and appears to be the nub of internal debate about Bulls-Eye cohesiveness.

Further, the keystone to building a reform agenda for New York State in the latter part of the 1990's is not just to maintain an exclusive group of Bulls-Eye districts. These districts need to be identified in organizational characteristics that make it easier for larger numbers of other districts with aspiring "exemplary secondary Regents programs" to strive for Bull-Eye status. If the Bulls -Eye group creates the "glue" of describing what high academic performance and k-12 organization mean together as exemplary practice, the "close" districts of New York State seem the next natural iteration for establishing grounds of commonalty.   The horizontal *keiretsu* of common identity and sentiment for articulating a mutual interest for reform actions depends upon evidence of a network of peers.

Multiple regression analyses were performed to profile the actual extent of systematic variation within the Bulls-Eye group. Final graduation and course performance created the dependent Points variable. Independent variables were consistent with descriptors presented in the Tables 2-3 to 2-6 above; tax rate per $1000 in 1993, full valuation per enrolled pupil in 1993, $CAADM in 1994, difference between revenues and expenditures without debt service in 1993, percent of spending for teaching and percent of spending for general support in 1993., Percent of state aid in 1993 and 1994 enrollment.
to the analyses.

The first regression determined the extent of significant variation within the Bulls-Eye group operating as a set of districts in the present (1993 and 1994). Analyses verified the Bulls-Eye group had important patterns of internal difference *but no overall statistically significant internal variation of descriptor variables* for the 1993-1994 time frame (F test score of 1.37 with a probability of .25). Individual descriptor relationships (beta coefficient measures) indicated the Points indice would exhibit statistically significant[9] variation with $CAADM and Full Valuation per enrolled child for the thirty three Bulls-Eye districts. The amount of internal variation accounted for by all descriptor relationships (using the rough approximate of correlation squared) was somewhat less than a third (.31) of all systematic patterning.

The second regression analysis of the Bulls-Eye Point dependent variable considered systematic patterns of changes over several years of time. Descriptors were change in tax rate per $1000 between 1990 and 1993, change in full valuation per enrolled pupil between 1990 and 1993, change in $CAADM between 1990 and 1994, change in teaching and general support allocations between fiscal year 1992 and fiscal year 1993, change in enrollment between 1990 and 1994 and change in percent of state aid between 1992 and 1993.

This multiple regression analysis of indices of changes over time also determined *no overall statistical significance* as an indication of internal variation (F test at 1.36 and probability of .26). The lack of important patterns of internal variations was further confirmed with analysis of individual indice relationships showed no beta coefficients with a t test value over 1.0.[10]

Multiple Regression Patterning to Individual Bulls-Eye Districts

A third perspective of the internal variation within the Bulls-Eye group can distinguish the relative positioning of individual districts. Although there were not statistically significant patterns of overall variation it is possible to distinguish individual districts by their multiple regression ranking with one another. Table 2-7 presents the rank ordering of the most extreme districts for both the present and over time analyses.

Table 2-7
Bulls-Eye District Regressions by Full Valuation and Spending per Child

At Present (not Significant)			**Over Time** (not Significant)		
District	Regression Score	Bulls-Eye Points	District	Regression Score	Bulls-Eye Points
Pleasantville	-12,5	4	Bryam Hills	-11.8	6
W. Irondequoit	-10.2	6	Pleasantville	-9.7	4
New Hartford	-7.1	5	New Hartford	-9.0	5
Elwood	-5.8	9	Great Neck	-8.0	11
Kings Park	-5.4	7	Port Jefferson	-7.9	7
Half Hollow Hill	-5.0	9	W. Irondequoit	-7.7	6
Syosset	+5.7	24	Syosset	+7.1	24
Rockville Ctr	+6.1	24	E. Willistone	+7.6	22
Clinton	+7.3	11	Mt. Sinai	+7.7	12
Fayetteville-Jame	+8.2	23	Cold Springs	+8.2	25
Jericho	+8.2	27	Rockville Ctr	+8.7	24
Garden City	+16.8	29	Garden City	+9.5	29

The policy implications framed by the three expressions of regression results would suggest there is an internal commonalty that can justify a general Bulls-Eye group classification. There does appear to be two subsets of districts that clustered in 1993-1994 by relatively high and low Points classification while sharing common descriptions of wealth capability and spending effort.

Conclusions

The thirty three k-12 jurisdictions that have the best college bound Regents secondary programs in New York State suggest an argument for possible horizontal *keiretsu* associations based upon their demonstration of exemplary practice. This conclusion would present the idea of high performance as quite an elite group of districts; less than five percent of the entire New York public school system. Closer study of the organizational characteristics of districts with excellent Regents secondary programs argues strongly that such k-12 school settings are comparatively rich, essentially inhabited by white students and located in the suburban "bedroom" communities surrounding New York State's big cities.

The "grassroots" organization association that might create the Bulls-Eye center of a reform network focused in some systemic way upon mastery criteria does seem to have a verifiable character. The next policy question is how such a centering group might relate to a much larger grouping of "close" jurisdictions and a multiple iteration configuration of viewing state wide reform.

---

[1] To gather authoritative data we must leave the academic performance information of educators and focus upon the fiscal data from the Office of State Comptroller. The shift in data sources has major implications for policy analysis. The Comptroller information is based upon the fiscal year instead of the academic year and k-12 education is reported as one organizational aspect of municipal government. The information of the Comptroller is always a year behind (e.g., the information for FY 1993 was released December 1994) because it represents the final, audited fiscal profile of public spending for the state.

[2] The tax levy includes the amount, if any, levied for a public library community college or senior high school in the district. A portion of the levy may be a "planned balance" to cover, in the succeeding year, expenditures between the opening of the school year and the receipt of property taxes. The percent of full value presents the tax levy as the tax rate per $1000 of full valuation and is calculated by moving the decimal point one place to the right. For example, a percent of full value of 1.398 would become the tax rate per $1000 of $13.98.

---

[3] debt service consists of principal and interest payments for the redemption of bonds and notes. These amounts may not include principal payments on short term indebtedness and bond anticipation notes.

[4] Comptroller's Special Report on Municipal Affairs, 1990, 1991, 1992, 1993

[5] The pupil measure is based upon average daily membership/enrollment and includes students enrolled in district programs, disabled students educated in district, BOCES, special section programs and students educated in other districts for which a district pays tuition. Prekindergarten and half day kindergarten pupils are weighed at 0.5.

[6] Comptroller, 1993 op cit pg. 325

[7] ibid

[8] In New York there are laws that protect the existing investments of "have" districts against dramatic redistributive politics. For example, the "save harmless" organization protect the current stipulation that no district can receive less money than the previous year. Similarly, there is an interest group protects the present arrangement that every district, no matter how rich, receives at least $360 per child as a "flat grant."

[9] .t-test analysis with level of confidence established at 95 percent or five chances out of one hundred that variation could have occured by chance alone.

[10] A second multiple regression it delimited to the relationship of three descriptors, points with full valuation and $CAADM indices, analyzed for the present and change over time. As expected, the re-analysis confirmed the statistically significant variation of the present condition among the three descriptors (F test of 2.2 with a probability of .03) for present time and over time (F Test value of 2.1 and probability of .04).

Chapter Four

The Addition of "Close" Districts to the Target Analogy

The target analogy takes shape rapidly when the decision rules are established to evaluate thresholds and, in turn, specific classifications are determined for particular k-12 districts. Point counting is automatic and so is the rank order placement of New York districts in relation to one another on secondary performance criteria.

Yet, the credibility of the target analogy only opens larger methodological issues of providing policy recommendations, especially how k-12 districts might operate exemplary secondary programs as a persistent state wide network. This chapter emphasizes both the Bulls-Eye districts to three rings of somewhat lesser exemplary performance that form a target of change opportunities and, second, the target to the four hundred plus other districts that receive some "close" points (those districts accumulating 3.5 to 0.5 points.). Special case analyses of the City District of New York, three secondary school districts and a possible clustering of k-12 districts in the "dim" area of the state's North Country will be discussed In the following chapter. [1]   Thirty three other k-12 jurisdictions are added to the thirty three Bulls-Eye districts to complete the target of exemplary Regents program districts. These additional target districts are identified by three iterations of point accumulation around the Bulls-Eye center: eight in the 7.0 to 5.5 "close" points or inner ring, six more in the 5.5 to 5.0 or middle ring and, finally, nineteen in the 4.5 and 4.0 count or the outer ring.

While each reader will have their own way of interpreting the State of New York as a target of k-12 district descriptions and reform possibilities, the core policy issue of jurisdictions demonstrating outstanding college bound, Regents focused secondary programs still depends upon fundamental decisions about definition and specification. [2]

One More Twist on the *Kieretsu* Idea

The difference between this chapter and the last is the difference between watching the teams playing the Super Bowl and understanding the concept of organizing to provide major league football. The performance of the two teams in January is verified and justified as the result of a season long testing process involving thirty teams. The organizational appreciation of all competing teams comes from understanding how performing is subdivided into the organized context of leagues, divisions and rank order finishes.

The relationship of investment in football stadiums, concessions and advertising for customers is analogous to (a)the continuing perception of the Board of Regents as an institutional authority, (b) the *demonstrated* ranking process of districts by secondary program results in degree production and nine subject areas and, indirectly,(c) improving curricular performance over time by using such Regents focused description of secondary school reform to rationalize alliance building among districts.

Because the costs of misunderstanding are great, we must approach cautiously the Japanese idea of *keiretsu* in creating a forum of horizontal networks. Asian and Western are different bases of thought and, like Thomas Jefferson's wavy wall of separation between America's version of church and state, we must traverse between the two cultures very deliberately. In terms of what has been discussed so far, horizontal *kieretsu* does seem to provide an organizational platform where fierce competition can be embedded within overall cooperation and collaboration of exemplary performance districts. Most important, the association *persists* in some lasting manner. However, cultural values vary across countries and parts of the world.[3] Westerners should appreciate that the fundamental "glue" of *keiretsu*, the idea that leadership should sustain group cohesiveness, has a distinctly Asian meaning.

> In the United States, a leader is usually someone with a strong ego, often with personal charisma, selected for his [or her] ability to make decisions, and to take responsibility with or without consulting his [her] associates. This kind of 'take charge' leader who wants to put his [her] stamp on the organization can be devastating to the Japanese because he [she] destroys the sense of harmony and consensus that is vital to the overall performance.[4]

"Take charge" Western analysts may have problems with this juxtaposition of apparently different concepts of culture when *persistence* of changing is the expectation. The issue is somewhat analogous to discussions of *kaizen* or "continuous improvement" as an generalized organizational phenomenon or a cultural derivative of distinctively Japanese social guidance.

The transfer of networking advice remains an unanswered question for predicting whether k-12 district educators in the metropolitan New York City region would accept long term trade-offs when the attainment of state specified cognitive and skill performance are pitted against specific district goals and involvement of particular communities. In a similar vein, the administrators, counselors and teachers working in the Capital region of New York may or may not share similar perceptions of what "proactive" agendas or "delivery" standards mean as general ideas of reform

These interpretations translate the Americanized context of interpersonal and politicized dynamics and create the acid tests for Japanese ideas of personal leadership styles and group harmony in networking. The end game of horizontal *keiretsu* relationships for New York State seems to center upon taking responsibility and being accountable to two distinct standards; the networked group of "target" districts and, simultaneously, belief about the long term legitimacy of the Regents program as state level criteria of evaluation for secondary "college bound" performance.

Consideration of adopting Japanese ideas suggests that both these commitments could, hypothetically, challenge the American notions of what success means to the individual and what personal choices can be made when sharing information with others in networking arrangments. Redmond infers the American twist to *kieretsu* relationships this way:

> Responsibility means that 'one is capable of making moral or rational decisions on one's own.' Westerners are more committed to taking responsibility because it *automatically* brings with it recognition and respect, regardless of consequent profit or loss, accorded to 'real persons.' But in [Asia] it is rank and its rewards that *gives the faint reading of responsibility* into the bargain. The honor is not the responsibility itself, but in the position that allows it to be borne. [5]

Borrowing ideas from different organizational cultures suggesting leadership approaches in various issue focused contexts does lead to murky policy descriptions. Yet, such effort also generates the possibilities of appreciating new networking and improvement strategies as a *tailored* policy agenda.

I would agree that vertical *keiretsu* associations are unlikely to break down the persistent determinism of superordinate and subordinate roles or the fixed shadings of expert to novice and senior to junior membership in decision making.[6]

Yet, horizontal *keiretsu*, borrowed and modified to the New York State context, might generate a network of agreements where responsibility and accountability for the processes of evaluating results rests with those people networking their views of public education. The results of working at the improvement of established Regents secondary programs for a semester or academic year may only create a "faint reading of responsibility" for the involved districts but it may be enough for educators already secure in their exemplary performance results. Basing discussion upon the patterning of performance results over an extended period of time (three to seven years collection) might facilitate speculations about translating future improvement into concrete, long term investment terms. Within the sharply delimited documentation of "college bound" intentions and the Regents program achievement results among exemplary districts important things can be said about the meaning of applied responsibilities for all districts operating advanced programs.

Building Networks of High Secondary Performance

New York State is a very large geographic area. Figure 3-1 suggests a pragmatic consideration of networking possibilities that imply an area or regional approach for initial contacts.

Figure 3-1
New York's Best Regents Points Producing* School Districts

	Nassau County		
Bulls-Eye	Inner Ring	Middle Ring	Outer Ring
Garden City	Bellmore .-Merrick(7.0)	Plainview(5.5)	Hewlett-Woodmere
Jericho		Sayville (6.0)	
Rockville Center		Southold (6.0)	
Syosset			
East Williston			
Roslyn			
Manhasset			
Herricks			
Great Neck			

	Suffolk County		
Bulls-Eye	Inner Ring	Middle Ring	Outer Ring
Cold Spring Harbor	Kings Park (7.0)	Harborsfields(5.0)	Shelter Island
Half Hollow Hills	Miller Place(7.0)	Smithtown (5.0)	Commack
Mt. Sinai	Port Jefferson(7.0)		Mattituck
Elwood			Shorham- Wading
Three Village			

Figure 3-1 Continued

	Westchester County		
Bulls-Eye	Inner Ring	Middle Ring	Outer Ring
Briarcliff Manor			Hasting on Hudson
Ardsley			Rye
Bryam Hills			
Pelham			
Pleasantville			

	Onondaga County		
Bulls-Eye	Inner Ring	Middle Ring	Outer Ring
Fayetteville-Manlius			
Westhill			
Jamesville-DeWitt			
Skateateles			

	Monroe County		
Bulls-Eye	Inner Ring	Middle Ring	Outer Ring
Pittsford		Penfield (5.0)	Fairport
West Irondequoit		Spencerport (5.0)	Honeoye Falls
			Gates Chili
			Brighton

	Broome County		
Bulls-Eye	Inner Ring	Middle Ring	Outer Ring
	Maine-Endicott (7.0)	Vestal (5.5)	Chenango Forks

	Lower Hudson Area		
Bulls-Eye	Inner Ring	Middle Ring	Outer Ring
	Clarkstown, Rockld. (7.0)	Spackenkill,Dutch	Nanuet,Rockland
			Mahopac,Putnam

	Capital Region Area		
Bulls-Eye	Inner Ring	Middle Ring	Outer Ring
North Colonie, Albany	Burnt Hills,Saratoga(6.0)		Chatham, Columbia
			Niskayuna, Schady

	Leather Stockings Area		
Bulls-Eye	Inner Ring	MIddle Ring	Outer Ring
Clinton, Oneida		Geneseo,Livi.(5.0)	Mohawk,Herkimer
New Hartford, Oneida			Cazenovia,Madison

	Western Area		
Bulls-Eye	Inner Ring	Middle Ring	Outer Ring
Amherst, Erie			East Aurora,Erie
Wayne, Wayne			

* "close" half point accumulation is presented in close caption or ( ) format.

A. On Long Island

Certainly, the largest concentration of top producing Regents secondary program districts in New York are located in Nassau and Suffolk counties on Long Island. Since World War Two, Long Island has been the major "bedroom community" for commuters to New York City. Westchester and Rockland counties to the north and northwest of the City also serve the "bedroom" function, but have a longer history of inhabitants that are not the result of postwar metropolitan growth.

Nassau County, the jurisdiction closest to New York City going out on the Island, can claim to be the county with the greatest concentration of k-12 districts with the most exemplary Regents secondary programs. A change strategy among the fifteen Nassau districts, identified by their exemplary performance, could create a "league" format consisting of several Bulls-Eye districts being part of a super division and other "close" point districts forming next best divisions.

In the same vein, the Bulls-Eye and Ring groups could make general agreements about the "college bound" focus and Regents orientation of secondary programs being offered. The horizontal network of Nassau's "lighthouse" districts then becomes the exchange arrangement for talking with other districts in adjacent counties and framing implications of state-wide policy.

Yet, this target group of k-12 districts may or may not be a direct influence on all jurisdictions in Nassau county. Educators in Nassau County know their county exhibits extreme differences in secondary performance among districts. There are, for example, seven Nassau districts with more than 100 pupils per square mile density that accumulated *no* exemplary or "close" points. Bellmore-Merrick district is a centtral high school jurisdiction serving four union free districts. We will also see in the special case situation discussion (Chapter Five) that three of these Nassau districts (with no accumulated points) are suburban jurisdictions with less than half the student body being white pupils. Given the reality that New York City failed to accumulate any exemplary or "close" points, and has nineteen percent white pupils averaged throughout the district, there seems no way to avoid the hypotheses of race to performance as an extension of City "urban" influences into Nassau county (and visa versa).

Suffolk County would seem to configure to a three league format of top producing or "lighthouse" Regents districts. Three Villages district of the Bulls-Eye group might be moved and added to the three districts of the next best inner ring (Kings Park, Miller Place, and Port Jefferson) while the middle and outer ring groups could be collapsed to a third group of six districts. If the thirteen exemplary districts of Suffolk county joined with the Nassau districts a horizontal *keiretsu* network of nearly thirty districts in two counties could form an "Island" meaning of Regents college bound implementation. However, like Nassau, Suffolk County also has nine districts with no point accumulation and three of these districts are suburban with less than fifty percent white pupils. Improvement of "college bound" programs within any particular county must appreciate the existing spectrum of actual performances that guide the plausibility of good or bad investments in systemic development of an area or region.

B. North of the City

Westchester County has a sharp division between the five exemplary Bulls-Eye districts and two outer ring "close" districts. Although there is the question of distance and geographic identity, a statewide model of building horizontal networks might join Hastings-on-Hudson and Rye districts from Westchester County with the four districts loosely identified in the "Lower Hudson Area." Certainly, Clarkstown and Nanuet districts from Rockland County and Mahopac district in Putnam County would share the metropolitan "bedroom" focus from New York City. Spackenkill district in Dutchess county is not proximate to the City, but could benefit from networking with the five other jurisdictions concerning Regents curriculum.

Despite the logic of such multiple county connection, there will likely be strong pressure for exemplary Westchester districts to not network. Westchester county has eight districts with more than 100 pupils per square mile density that earned no exemplary or close points. Five of these districts are formally designated city jurisdictions (Yonkers, Peekskill, White Plains, New Rochelle and Mount Vernon) and three other jurisdictions earning no points have student bodies with less than fifty percent white pupils (Greenburgh, Tarrytowns, Port Chester). The political intensity of such intra-county difference in secondary performance may guarantee only an indirect, introspective look by Westchester policy makers.

C. Metropolitan Areas Around Syracuse, Rochester, Binghamton

The New York counties of Onondaga, Monroe and Broome house most of the metropolitan area surrounding the cities of Syracuse, Rochester and Binghamton respectively. While these three areas have fifteen of the districts that are identified as the center or one of the three rings of high producing Regents districts, the analogy of a complete target of producers is only partially developed.

In the Syracuse area (Onondaga county) there are four Bulls-Eye jurisdictions but no districts in the three iterations. Monroe county (the Rochester area) has two Bulls-Eye districts and six more jurisdictions in the middle and outer ring identification.

The Binghamton area (Broome county) has no Bulls-Eye district, but one each in the three rings. Broome county would probably fare best with Maine-Endicott, Vestal and Chenango Forks districts forming a horizontal relationship.

In Monroe county (Rochester area) Pittsford district seems to stand alone, while the other Bulls-Eye district, West Irondequoit, could join and link with the six jurisdictions in the middle and outer ring classification.

D. the Capital, the Leather Stocking and Western Part of State

In the Capital region of the state, North Colonie districts stands head and shoulders above the rest of the Regents oriented, college bound programs.   Unlike the relationship with Pittsford district in Monroe county, North Colonie in Albany county may provide a crucial inter-county linkage with Burnt Hills district in Saratoga county, Chatham district in Columbia county and Niskayuna district in Schenectady county.

A similar inter-county relationship seems to exist between Clinton district in Oneida county and four other districts in the Leather Stockings area of the state; New Hartford district of Oneida county, Geneseo district of Livingston county, Cazenovia district of Madison county and Mohawk district of Herkimer county.   While each of these district share natural contacts with other jurisdictions in their county, the potentials for leading a four county change initiative also seems feasible.

For those readers expecting New York State to reflect a general conclusion that exemplary college bound, Regents programs proliferate in suburbs around large cities, the Western part of the state may prove a disappointment.   Although Buffalo City district is the second largest k-12 jurisdiction in the state (46,000+ pupils) and more than forty districts are in the Buffalo metropolitan area, only Amherst (home of SUNY Buffalo) and East Aurora districts within Erie county, and Wayne district located in Wayne county, would be included in the target analogy.

The Hourglass Analogy of Distinctive New York Conditions

There is also a distinctive culture of educational politics that must be factored into any strategy for promoting horizontal *keiretsu* associations within New York State. The analogy is an hourglass of political expectations that would result in pressuring any new networking effort to coordinate in the "middle."   At one end of the hourglass are the relationships of k-12 districts with New York's intermediate governments or Boards of Cooperative Educational Services (hereafter BOCES). Decades long associations between districts and BOCES governments cannot be significantly challenged or replaced by a new network of exemplary districts. Certainly the services of some BOCES agencies to individual districts exceeds what the State Education Department, the Governor's Office or any major university offered in terms of high quality contracted services.[7]

Yet, in the mid 1990's, BOCES and county jurisdictions are occasionally in conflict over the provision of "shared or linked" services to a particular district.[8] Many disagreements also result over the contractual benefits of certain state aid related services (e.g., special education) and the uncertainty created when the State Education Department mandates a BOCES consolidation or new regional arrangment. If New York State continues its Compact for Learning tendency to think of the secondary education obligation to "career" and "employability" foci (e.g. industry partnerships and economic development zones, school-to-work programs and high school-community college "tech prep" efforts) local district interpretations of the "college bound" Regents curriculum will remain a question mark.

At the other end of the hourglass is the pragmatic reality of the cumulative effect of promoting decentralized operations to the point where many individual districts prefer to "do their own thing." In the mid 1990's the Compact for Learning encouragement of Shared Decision-Making by mandate for direct community involvement and formal committeesseems to have, paradoxically, reinforced the "egg crate" culture of bureaucratic isolation for the teacher professional.

If, for example, local teachers perceive that "Curriculum Frameworks" from the state are not bridging the *multiple logics* of college bound and career bound expectations in their particular community, they will likely retreat into the self contained "crate" of their classroom and do nothing differently. There seems to be little of the "implicit normative structures that help to organize new policy systems"[9] emerging from the shared decision making experiences.

It might be argued that the national controversy over the meanings of "school delivery standards, " "opportunity to learn" assessments and "high stakes" investments have also contributed to individual districts less inclined to work with other jurisdictions. Certainly the idea of Opportunity To Learn in federal legislation surrounding Goals 2000 became a political firestorm around the whole meaning of standards and school productivity.[10] No one can predict the extent that national or federal controversy has a dampening effect upon local perceptions of participation and involvement. It seems fair to speculate, however, in a political climate where some State Boards are turning down Goals 2000 moneys for technology because of fears of federal "mind control" (e.g. in neighboring New Hampshire) that local districts may be less inclined to network and create a highly visible profile.

Finally, the focus upon teacher interpretation in discussing organized delivery and meanings of opportunity to learn or what is considered a high stakes in classrooms may also contribute to an inward looking by individual districts. There is a fear that opportunity to learn standards coupled to conventional meanings of productivity standards could lead to litigation on civil rights violation grounds. In 1994, the high school exit examinations in Ohio were investigated by the Office of Civil Rights to determine whether minority students were being provided the opportunity to learn the content on the state test.

The Target Analogy and the Rest of the "Close" District Population

The sixty six districts identified as part of the center or three iteration target of New York high performers are embedded in a pool of 464 districts that achieved some measure of Regents point accumulation. The target analogy identifed Bulls-Eye and those "close" districts who achieved 4.0 or better points.

The total pool of point accumulating districts achieved at least one one-half point in some Regents based performance during the three years of analysis (1990-1991 through 1993-1994). Seventy one percent of all k-12 districts in the state were identified as having some Regents points by this type of evaluation.

Each day, approximately 1,057,000 New York school aged children get educated in such districts. Assuming the secondary program is approximately one-fourth of the entire k-12 enrollment, slightly over one-quarter of a million pupils (264,000) are responsible for generating these exemplary performance data. The reader may wish to quickly review Appendices A through J to get a sense of the proportions allowed in judging different meanings of "close" ratios for individual Regents subjects and particular district's "close" half point accumulations.

Table 3-1 illustrates clearly that the addition of the Bulls-Eye districts to the entire point accumulating district population only makes minor changes in the demographic profile of statewide averages.

We can speculate that New York districts making a strong effort to improve their Regents secondary programs are slightly smaller than the state average in enrollment and pupil density, pay the same average tax rate per $1000 full assessment and distribute the actual spending of resources across teaching, administration, general support and transportation much like the state average district.

Table 3-1
Demographics of "Close" Districts in 1993-1994

Characteristics	Only "Close	"Close & Bulls-Eye	State wide
	n=434	n=459*	n=649
k-12 Enrollment (average)	2239	2288	2547
Pupil/Sq Mile (density)	133.4	144.3	153.1
Regents Diploma %	44.4	45.7	42.9
College Bound intentions	77.3	78.3	76.4
Secondary Dropout %	1.9	1.8	2.1
Combined Wealth Ratio	.98	1.03	.96
% Free/Reduced Lunches	26.4	25.2	29.2
Census Poverty Classification	9.2	8.8	10.3
Tax Rate per $100	$14.21	$14.22	$14.14
Full Value per Enrolled Child	390,600	407,200	375,700
% State Aid (average)	42%	41%	44%
% Federal Aid (average)	3%	3%	4%
% spent on direct teaching	60%	60%	60%
% spent on administration	6%	7%	6%
% spent on LEA support	6%	6%	6%
% spent on transportation	6%	6%	6%

• iincludes nine Bulls-Eye districts with "close" and mastery points

One distinguishing feature is the greater wealth capability of the Bulls-Eye and "Close" districts when assessed by combined wealth ratio (for determining percent of state aid), percent of free and reduced lunches and the full valuation per enrolled child. There is no way to avoid the political ramifications of greater wealth and exemplary Regents performers in New York State.

"Close" Differences in Regents Subjects and Graduation Rates

Exploring the pool of jurisdictions that accumulated at least one one-half point for "close" ratios (between 0.5 and 1.5 during three years) provides a graduation rate and subject by subject analysis of the "close" districts.   For the three years of study any New York district could generate 1.5 times the 60/85 graduation criteria and nine subjects for 15.0 total "close" points. The target of exemplary performance removes those "close" districts with Bulls-Eys status and those between 7.0 and 4.0 half point scores to create a remaining subpopulation of districts between 3.5 and 0.5 points.

To study the internal patterning of this remaining "close" district population (61 percent of the entire state wide model) on a subject by subject basis, we note the simple regression effect when the pattern of one subject is compared to district performance in graduation and all remaining eight subjects. In Table 3-2 we find that neither the relationship to full 60/85 graduation point nor the relationship to "close" 60/85 point accumulation are statistically significant.

Table 3-2
Patterns of "Close" Districts by Regents Subject Performance, 1990-1994

Subject	N=	RSq	Intercept	Slope	F Test	t Test	Probability
Rd/CB "Full"	38	.07	3.028	.70	2.71	1.64	.10
Rd/CB "Close"	92	.02	2.188	.82	1.84	1.35	.17
Hist/Govt	117	.11	1.034	2.07	15.26	3.90	.0002*
Global	142	.04	1.151	1.26	6.33	2.51	.01*
French	46	.004	1.182	.81	0.18	0.43	.66
Spanish	168	.06	0.913	1.28	11.80	3.43	.0007*
Interm. Math	133	.33	0.065	3.68	66.27	8.14	.0001*
Advance Math	59	.04	1.370	3.00	2.91	1.70	.09
Biology	116	.21	0.342	3.08	30.84	5.55	.0001*
Chemistry	45	.18	0.904	3.64	9.66	3.10	.003*
Physics	91	.04	1.470	1.43	4.62	2.14	.03*

* statistically significant at .05 or better

The regression analysis gives a rough estimate of the amount of systematic variance accounted for (correlation squared or RSq.), a F score generated by analysis of variance, a t test based upon beta coefficients and a probability assignment of found versus expected relationships in a random situation.

The larger the probability determination of a relationship not happening by simple chance(from .05 through .0001), the more likely that the pattern of particular districts found in one subject are systematically projected to some other Regents subjects.

The pattern of "close" districts in French is unrelated to the patterning of other subjects while, in contrast, the pattern of "close" districts in History/ Government, Spanish, Intermediate Mathematics and Biology are very much a study of systematic variations.

Curricular Networking

While there is some suggestion of connecting by subject in the science area (e.g. Biology, Chemistry and Physics all indicating statistically significant patterning), the four subjects most indicative of possible common tendencies in performance are History/ Government, Spanish, Intermediate Math and Biology.   Figure 3-2 describes a potential reform agenda of networking districts by county or region to a common subject reference.

Figure 3-2
Best Performing Counties by "Close" Points in Four Regents Subjects

County	Hist/Gov	Spanish	I nterm Math	Biology
Nassau County	16(2)/56*		15(5)/56	15(4)/56
Suffolk County	24(5)/68			
Westchester County	14(1)/38			14(2)/38
Monroe County		9/18		
Onondaga County			7(2)/18	
Erie County		11(1)/28	9(1)/28	
Rockland County		7/8		
Albany County		5/12		
Schenectady County			3/6	
Oneida County		5/16		
Ontario County			7/9	
Alleghany County		6/14		
Jefferson County	4/11			4/11
St. Lawrence County			5/17	5/17

* the number of k-12 districts in a county, not the total number of districts. Districts also identified in the Bulls-Eye center are listed in parentheses ( ).

For those strategizing how to improve the Regents secondary programs between the present and the 21st Century, the relative numbers of "close" districts give a gross estimate of "best bet" investments. For example, the intermediate mathematics program within Ontario county appears to be on the threshold of general improvement. Seven of the nine districts in the county are "close" to the exemplary thresholds established in this analysis. Rockland county districts have approximately the same situation for Spanish.

Attempting to establish a horizontal *keiretsu* discussion in the New York City area, suburban counties would seem to initiate questions of History/Government curricular performance. Spreading the wealth of involvement might argue that less than half the districts in Nassau, Suffolk or Westchester counties are identified as "close" in this subject area, but five of Suffolk's Bulls-Eye jurisdictions are listed.

Suffolk may take the lead in the History/Government area in exchange for Nassau county districts leading in the Intermediate Mathematics subject and Westchester taking the lead in conversations about Biology.   For state level policy makers concerned about the remote, rural areas of up-state, the curricular situation in Jefferson and St. Lawrence counties seem a feasible starting point for horizontal networking. In Jefferson county, the districts of LaFargeville, General Brown and Carthage are found in both the History/Government and Biology "close" jurisdictions. In St. Lawrence county, the districts of Herman-DeKalb, Madison and Potsdam are listed for both the Intermediate Mathematics and Biology subjects.

Remaining Districts With No Points

The final story of New York State districts concerns the 190 jurisdictions that scored niether degree production nor Regents subject points during the three years under study. Twenty nine percent of the districts throughout the state enrolling more than 605,000 children would be identified as receiving no points. New Yorkers appreciate that the size of the student population receiving education in no point districts exceeds a large number of state k-12 educational systems around the nation (eg. neighboring Vermont has 93,000 children enrolled in all k-12 arrangements).

The key issue of applied methodology revolves around whether there is a substantive difference between the 190 districts operating with no points and those 459 districts receiving some points. The issue of reform implementation within the group of no point districts is whether there is a bimodal distribution of dense populated (over 100 children per square mile) and remote populated (under 15 pupils per square mile) jurisdictions?

It is obvious that large city school systems throughout New York State (Buffalo, Syracuse, Rochester, Yonkers, Mount Vernon, Newburgh, Utica) are within the no points grouping. The possibility of Regents secondary improvement being directly related to basic questions of large city schooling, racial composition of the student body and academic performance are discussed in the special case situations (in the following chapter). Certainly, the initial "nation at risk" reform agenda sustained throughout the 1980's was concentrated upon the plight of secondary programs in urban or city school systems.[11]

Table 3-3 describes the demographic profile between "no points" districts, target districts and the state "average" district. No point districts differ from districts within the "points" target analogy and the average jurisdiction in the 649 model in general wealth capacity. Combined wealth ratio is a New York State formula for distributing educational state aid to individual districts. The calculation of a personal income and property tax incomes for citizens in each district establishes a rough baseline for the state's contribution.

We can see that there is considerable difference between point and no point identification when districts are compared on general percent of state and federal aid received, percent of free and reduced lunch aid received and, particularly, the assessed full value per enrolled child.

Table 3-3
"No Point," "Point" and the "Average" K-12 State District (1993-1994 Data)

Characteristics	"No Point"	"Close & Bulls-Eye	State wide
	n=190	n=459	n=649
k-12 Enrollment (average)	3185	2288	2547
Pupil/Sq Mile (density)	175.7	144.3	153.1
Regents Diploma %	36.7	45.7	42.9
College Bound intentions	71.7	78.3	76.4
Secondary Dropout %	2.9	1.8	2.1
Combined Wealth Ratio	0.77	1.03	0.96
% Free/Reduced Lunches	38.8	25.2	29.2
Census Poverty Classification	13.7	8.8	10.3
Tax Rate per $1000	$14.00	$14.22	$14.14
Full Value per Enrolled Child	299,400	407,200	375,700
% State Aid (average)	51%	41%	44%
% Federal Aid (average)	5%	3%	4%
% spent on direct teaching	60%	60%	60%
% spent on administration	6%	7%	6%
% spent on LEA support	6%	6%	6%
% spent on transportation	6%	6%	6%

A core policy question about academic performance in any curriculum is the extent to which equity values are also expressed in efforts to reform the present condition. If the networking attempt to improve secondary programs throughout New York State is to be successful educators in districts with no points must be convinced that Regents excellence is more than having an abundance of riches to support an elite program.

Table 3-4 describes the internal distribution of the no points group expressed as a bimodal distinction of districts located in sparsely and densely populated areas. Remember that the percentages for general support, administration, instruction and transportation were generated from Office of Comptroller data with debt service amounts removed.

According to the Comptroller definition, *the Administration category is related to the costs to support instruction* (not equipment) and defined as "expenditures for curriculum development and supervision of regular and special schools, research, planning and evaluation, in-service training, school library, audio-visual, educational television and computer assisted instruction." The general support category is defined as "expenditures for such items as board of education, district clerk, chief school officer, tax collection, legal, central data processing, special items such as judgments and claims and other support services.

Table 3-4[12]
Within the "No-Point" Subpopulation, Comparing the Total Subpopulation
With Over 100 and Less Than 15 Pupils per Square Mile Districts

Characteristic	"All No Point"	"Over 100 "	"Less Than 15"
# districts	n=190	n=54	n=68
# students affected	605,000	361,000	74,500
k-12 Enrollment (average)	2288	6690	1080
Pupil/Sq Mile (density)	144.3	566.5	8.18
Regents Diploma %	45.7	32.1	36.5
College Bound intentions%	78.3	76.5	66.7
Secondary Dropout %	1.8	3.4	2.6
Combined Wealth Ratio	1.03	0.95	0.66
% Free/Reduced Lunches	25.2	44.6	40.2
Census Poverty Classification[13]	8.8	14.9	15.5
Tax Rate per $1000	$14.22	15.24	13.12
Full Value per Enrolled Child	407,200	327,700	326,100
% State Aid (average)	41%	.41	.56
% Federal Aid (average)	3%	5%	5%
% spent on direct teaching	60%	61%	60%
% spent on administration	6%	7	5
% spent on general LEA support	6%	5	7
% spent on transportation	6%	5	6

An interesting comparative policy question for internal analysis of "no points" district population would be to compare dense and sparse jurisdictions about the institutional relationships of spending money to administer instruction directly and for general managing of the district jurisdiction. While such comparison would not resolve the "site-based" versus "district" questions of governance, it could clarify how administration of instruction differs between, for example, spending on curricular development and library or educational television and research.

Summary

The analogy of talking about a Bulls-Eye center and three rings of exemplary secondary performance as a "target" for reforming New York State is found in the identity of sixty six k-12 districts as high performing public service institutions. The state wide pool of nearly 460 districts who achieved some Regents point count show the potential of seven out of ten districts for immediate secondary improvement through emphasis on the Regents program.

As a strategy for state wide reform the issue of using mastery standards to identify curriculum performance faces daunting challenges. While I have argued that the Regents allows New Yorkers to reemphasize the *state* identity, there is little question that the emphasis on national standards and the role of the federal government in Goals 2000 legislation will create major identity problems for any networking effort.

There are strong pressures against any form of standards or measures of school productivity. These may be coupled with ideologically driven reactions against the idea of public schools or could be coming from misunderstanding of the Compact for Learning intentions. Certainly extreme decentralization of school accountability does not absolve public educators from their professional responsibility to have all children become literate and achieve in an academic sense. Local control never meant a negation of responsibility to deliver a public service.

The potential for misunderstanding in the mid 1990's is demonstrated with the challenges to the idea of "educational outcomes" on one hand and the "delivery of services" on the other. As an pure intellectual argument few people would argue against the premise that the content and performance aspects of Regents productivity should also make specific concession to the delivery system that operates to promote such productivity. It is one kind of policy concern to worry whether individual subjects are "interdisciplinary" enough to meet tests of coherence and quite another to worry whether any subject is being taught in school settings so disadvantaged or impoverished that children do not have a chance to learn.

The issue is when delivery system is defined as standards to assess as opposed to strategies to improve. The national debate over the former controversy translated into Opportunity to Learn standards when defined as;

> the criteria for, and the basis of, assessing the sufficiency and quality of the resources, practices, and conditions necessary at each level of the education system (schools, districts, states) to provide all students with the opportunity to learn the material in voluntary national content standards [14]

With this effort to identify specific sets of school districts by the accumulation of Regents point count reformers of secondary education in New York State have a specific rationale for identification of "best bet" k-12 jurisdictions throughout the state. They also have a rationale to identify 190 districts where non productivity could raise the possibility of "high stakes" situations and inadequate delivery systems.

Assuming the idea of local districts networked in alliances of horizontal *keiretsu* relationships, where demonstrated academic performance is the major determinant of identity, is it possible to imagine such networks defining the institutional parameters of opportunity to learn? In New York State, with the Regents secondary curriculum as a guide, the chances seem good at the low stakes end (e.g. the Bulls-Eye proven performers) and more problematic but still possible at the high stakes (e.g. no points districts) end .

Sufficiency and quality of resources are two very different types of policy considerations. Certainly, sufficiency involves a theory of the appropriate distribution of social goods [15] while quality must concede the perceptions of the client or customer being delivered to. [16] Neither can be adequately presented as an aggregate phenomenon, especially from the national or international level of government.

Networks of districts throughout New York State might have a chance to compare and contrast their conclusions about meanings of opportunities to learn *if such meanings were derived from a long process of networked association and politically conscious deliberation.* There are regional differences throughout New York State and this difference is as real as the criteria of Regents performance that distinguishes sixty six districts from one hundred and ninety districts. Networking arrangements create the potential forums to reach conclusions about contextual embedded meanings of what is sufficient and what is qualitative in the delivery operations of secondary schooling as it now exists. The problem is that some people will dislike the conclusions reached. the hope is that the conclusions reached by individual networks would form the grounds for some negotiated understandings where New York educators and citizens rebind the values of accommodation and compromising. The irony of using the Regents as a vehicle to achieve such a forum rather than an anti-Regents argument to dream of a brand new world is the sugar in the coffee.

From a state wide perspective, the Bulls-Eye and Target networks may resemble a confederation of vested interests that are too mosaic like to satisfy traditional perspectives of overall unity. I think that is the price of public education operations in the mid to late 1990's. We might yearn for a more federated, unified system of commonalty but, in the secondary schools at least, the tide is running the other direction.

Certainly the "politics of inclusion" over multiculturalism ranks with the Reagan "bully pulpit" in demonstrating that exhortation and praying for "osmosis like" changes will not be strong enough for the New York State future. Networking processes in operation can create a meaning of state wide system as a lattice form of sub organizations. The web of alliances may be the only viable way to approach the knotty issues of inequity and, possibly, overt discrimination. Certainly, using the Regents standard for identification forces all New Yorkers to recognize that more than 600,000 students attend public schools in No Point districts(not counting New York City district).

The politics of documenting exemplary "college bound" performance for some jurisdictions also makes the case for state policy makers that children in one-fourth of all New York's districts do not have such an environment. Documenting these kinds of pragmatic realizations in an extended accounting of district performance sets the stage for networking between the present have and have not situations. What potitical concession guarantees is that all involved will appreciate that using indicators is a value laden activity and data can document ideologically driven interpretations of such information.[17] For example, a network of associated districts could create their own meanings of what procedural fairness means or when compensation differs from redistribution to achieve a perfromance level. The hope would be that Regents mastery standards, as determinants of achievement outcomes, also become a point of departure to discuss "close" district efforts and collective reform strategies to network delivery of services for all jurisdictions.

---

[1] An initial format for comparing New York City district performance to the "rest of the state" might reverse political correctness and focus upon racial composition of student body. There are fifteen k-12 districts with less than 50 percent of enrolled students being Caucasian(see Chapter Five). If race of pupils is not the primary determinant, the fifty four "no points" districts with an urban density of 100 pupils per square mile or greater could be a more subtle comparison.

[2] It is less inclusion in the grouping than the fact that each perspective can generate different and interesting speculations about systemic change orientations with specific strategies for implementation of improvement efforts. See William Clune, " Educational Policy in an Era of Uncertainty; or, How to Put Eggs in Different Baskets" in Fuhrman and Malen(ed) The Politics of Curriculum and Testing, 1991, pages 125-138. Also Richard Townsend and Norman Robinson, "Making Politics of Education Even More Interesting" in Jay Scribner and Donald Layton(ed) The Study of Educational Politics, 1995, pages 185-200.

[3] discussed as "instructional guidance" within the context of existing organizational arrangments in David Cohen and James Spillane, " Policy and Practice: The Relations of Governance and Instruction in Nina Cobb(ed) The Future of Education (New York: College Board) 1995, pages 143-149

[4] Phillip Hallinger,"Culture and Leadership" Educational Considerations S pring 1995, pg. 10

[5] Charles Redmond, "The Unselfishness of Not Being There," cited in T. Rohlen, "The Order of Japanese Society: Attachment, Authority and Routine" Journal of Japanese Studies, 15, 1989, page 29. Note that Redmond was talking about Thailand culture in Asia and not Japan.

Policy Research in Education) 1984. Also Susan Fuhrman <u>Standardization Admidst Diversity</u> (New Brunswick: Center for Policy Research in Education) May 1989

[7] Compare, for example, the State's Technology Network rationale for statewide technology linkages to be developed over a ten year period to what the Suffolk and Nassau BOCES created in one year as a descriptive profile of existing school-linked services and shared service arrangements. While the state effort was a proposed "action plan" the "local" BOCES initiative made substantive contribution to actual policy developments in local districts .

[8] Two state level agendas that have been particularly confusing to the BOCES-local district relationship are the school linked services that involve counties and the efforts to merge or consolidate existing BOCES into larger units in upstate New York.

[9] Tom James has argued that the generative concepts of individual differences, differenetiated curriculum and fiscal neutrality have played a central role in shaping educational policy. The same cannot be said of shared decsion making. See Tom James, "State Authority and the Politics of Educational Change," <u>Review of Research in Education</u> , 17, 1991, pages 169-224.

[10] Andrew Porter, "The Uses and Misuses of Opportunity-to-Learn Standards" <u>Educational Researcher</u> 24, 1995, pages 21-27, Lorraine McDonnell, "Opportunity to Learn as a Research Concept and Policy Instrument" <u>Educational Evaluation and Policy Analysis,</u> 17, Fall 1995, pages 305-322.

[11] Ronald Edmunds research into "effective schools" provided the rationale for much of the "nation at risk" reform response and program improvement efforts. In the mobilization of state wide reform efforts it was assumed that the Edmund research results, based upon his observations of elementary schools in large city systems, were applicable to all schools in all settings. See " Some Schools Work and More Can" <u>Social Policy</u>, 1979, pages 28-32. Also <u>Discussion of the Literature and Issues Related to Effective Schooling</u> (ERIC ED 170 394) 1980

I believe that actual consideration of "effective school organizations" can be traced to the late 1960's. See Metfessel and Michael, " A Paradigm involving Multiple Criterion Measures.in the Evaluation of Effectiveness in School Programs" <u>Educational and Psychological Measurement</u>, 1967, pages 931-943.

[12] Table 3-4 may contain most important information to appraise local education institutions in overlooked locations and operating academically discounted secondary curriculums. A September 1995 conference sponsored by the National Center for Educational Statistics and other interests in "informing rural education policy as we translate data into decisions"(conference title) was concerned about finance and performance of rural school systems. The "less than 15" group of sixty eight No Point districts was further delimited to 53 jurisdictions and compared to 53 Points districts with the same "less than 15" characteristic. The academic performance of secondary students in "less than 15" districts continues to be a "curricular capability" concern, especially in places like New York State where the secondary programs failed to generate any full Regents points.

[13] The use of School District Data Base information about children aged 5 through 17 years (hence the name SDDB SubPopulation) allowed, for the first time, in-depth analysis of New York State Education Department classification of counties as disaggregated official 1990 socio-economic district characteristics. The Census data directly formatted to district level (in CD-ROM disk formt, developed by The Mesa Group) was analyzed as relative rish and poor Census Poverty Index jurisdicitons within the SDDB Subpopulation.

[14] Conference Report on HR 1804 Goals 2000: Educate America Act, 1994 <u>Congressional Record</u> 140, H1625-H1664

[15] Gretchen Guiton and Jeanne Oakes, "Opportunity to Learn and Concepttions of Educational Equality, " <u>Educational Evaluation and Polcy Analysis,</u> 17, Fall 1995 pages 323-336

[16] Micheal Smith and Jennifer O'Day "Systemic School Reform" in Susan Fuhrman and Betty Malen, <u>Politics of Curriculum and Testing, Politics of Education Yearbook</u>, (New York: Falmer) 1990, pages 233-267

[17] Guiton and Oakes <u>op cit.</u> suggest that opportunity to learn indicators present very different interpretations of equity to the libertarian, liberal and democratic liberal analyst.

Chapter Five

Networking in Special Case Situations

Creating the rationale for a statewide model of k-12 district performance expressed in college bound secondary programs is both a ..methodological exercise and a pragmatic mapping of existing arrangements. In our enthusiasm for setting delimitation on the group being analyzed and mastery thresholds for general goal and/or standards expectations, it is possible to lose touch with the pragmatic "dalliance" of operating real secondary school programs.

This study has emphasized that the methodology processes focus our deliberate consideration of New York public education, especially as a statewide system of k-12 public school districts. In this study, the pragmatic reality of New York State has been altered from a operating system of 718 district jurisdictions to a state wide model of approximately 650 units for analysis.

Although the created model includes nine of ten districts throughout the state, policy makers concerned with real life are continuously affected by the remaining ten percent (some would claim that there is an overly serious preoccupation with that missing percentage).

The spirit of *keiretsu* for considering a systemic networking improvement of all secondary school programs in New York State demands clarification of the intellectual bridges linking change efforts and extrapolations from the model data. In this chapter, three special case situations are discussed in light of a full and pragmatic meaning of instituting *state wide* improvement of college bound public education.

The City of New York District

The City district of New York, home to more than a quarter of a million secondary school students, presents the strongest case for discussing the "college bound Regents" implications of academic performance in situations with many high schools and much internal variation. New York City is composed of five boroughs and the many high schools in each borough are reported in aggregate summary fashion to the state.[1] In the last chapter we noted that comparison of districts with a single high school to those jurisdictions with more than one school creates possible methodological questions.

When the results of "target" districts throughout the state are implied to have meaning for the secondary programs operating in New York City district there must be a concurrent pragmatic consideration of that special situation. The City of New York district does reflect the state wide tendency for growing percentages of seniors to indicate "college bound" intentions at the same time percentage of graduates with Regents diplomas has declined. Further, the City district would join with the 190 districts identified in this study as having a "no point" condition for nine Regents courses.

Because the tidal wave of sensationalism generated in recent reporting of big city school academics as fundamentally a study of race and poverty,[2] New York City district must be speculated upon in racial - specific and several sociological terms.

The pragmatist writer has two options to approach such a politically sensitive consideration. One path of assessment leads to the fifteen k-12 districts with less than fifty percent of their enrolled student body being white.[3]   As most of these districts are coterminous to the City in the larger metropolitan area of "down state," state level policy makers might make regional inferences about linking school improvement efforts to this subset of the entire state model under question. The second path leads to the somewhat safer consideration of fifty four "no points" districts with a pupil density of 100 students/ per square mile. While tempting from a Robert Frost poem perspective, I choose to take a short break from either alternative while others play through.

A portion of this chapter on policy implications of taking reform initiatives in New York State is devoted to districts with less than 15 pupils per square mile. The point and no point "sparcity" districts demand full attention within the large forest of "remoteness," "rural" and "non-metropolitan" policy concerns.   So the two paths will be traversed at another time while others clear the way through the deep thickets of "density," "urban" and "metropolitan" referenced politics. In either setting, lack of contextual appreciation leads to over blown sociological classifications as they substitute for real knowledge about people in organizations.[4]   For those particularly concerned with policy comparisons to New York City interests, the minimum density limit could also be raised *for comparative purposes* to a subgroup of districts with 750 pupils/ square mile. One can only hope to shake hands with or stand on the shoulders of those academic players who resolve the "greater than 100" versus "greater than 750" comparisons of "urban" settings.

Figure 4-1 lists the other "no points" districts state wide that could be included in such designation opportunities should the need for a mediating "3rd" party arise..

Figure 4-1
"No Points" k-12 Districts Exceeding 750 Pupil Square Mile

Nassau County	Suffolk County	Westchester	Rest of State
•Freeport	Babylon	Peekskill	Binghamton
•Hempstead	Bay Shore	•Port Chester	Buffalo
Mineola	•Brentwood	•Tarrytowns	Cohoes
Plainedge	•Central Islip		Poughkeepsie
•Roosevelt	Lindenhurst		Rochester
Westbury	Middle Country		Schenectady
	South Huntington		Syracuse
	•Wyandach		Townowanda
			Watervliet

• = enrolled students less than 50 percent white

The pragmatic policy speculation about the City would include the questions of whether educators believe their local secondary curriculum is superior to the state regulated Regents curriculum for "college bound" students and whether the assessment of "no points" means a mediocre secondary program or rejection of the Regents course sequence and the particular Regents graduation credential.

Of course, I realize the risk of being interpreted as politically incorrect or even suggesting that linkage between institutions consider the proportion of nonwhite student populations. The peek attempted here would be a preliminary step to look harder at the question of *local* challenges to secondary Regents programs rather than the end game of a strategic plan to recreate a segregated "white/ nonwhite" world of 1950's policy vintage. Once racial composition of the student body is looked at as an important component of organizational complexity, the stage is set to weave back through some of the most blatant indictments. The argument that fiscal discrimination are found in city or "urban" district secondary programs, and that such patterning is due to the "racist" format of Regents secondary education, seems a good place to start.

Let the debate proceed with the proviso of the "equity" and "democracy" controversies discussed earlier. The marvelous to outrageous "marketplace of ideas" needs embedding in pragmatic discussions about the policy environment, but it is mandatory where discussion is about secondary learning taking place in compulsory public service institutions.

Special Secondary Only School Districts

The second special situation concerns the three secondary school district jurisdictions in New York State deliberately left out of this study and statewide modeling effort. The three schools-as-districts are part of the, roughly, forty districts with less than a full k-12 complement of grades. The special secondary program districts were eliminated from this institutionally focused expression of k-12 type organizations in a state wide model even though the secondary curriculum relationship to Regents programs is as pertinent to these peculiar jurisdictions as any other in the state.

As a partial concession to the larger idea of linking school improvement efforts in all secondary school setting, Sewanhaka district in Nassau county was identified as a comparative illustration. This particular jurisdiction is much larger than the average enrollment of the Bulls-Eye or other exemplary "target" k-12 districts, with more than 6600 pupils in the secondary program alone. This district also had the relatively unusual demographic characteristics of 65 percent white pupil population (in 1993-1994) and a 1990 Census poverty ranking of two(indicating a high wealth capability).

For the 1993-1994 academic year Sewanhaka district would not have met the 60/85 percent threshold for Bulls Eye or exemplary point Regents production. The district, would however, have likely classified for a "close" point jurisdiction with a performance demonstration of 49.6 percent Regents degree graduates and 88.6 percent of seniors indicating a "college bound" future.

New York State's Dim Areas

The third special case condition leads to consideration of trying to improve Regents secondary education in the "dim" parts of the state. Dim parts of New York State are areas where Regents focused state level policy analysis registers large numbers of "no points" districts and few "point" districts. In the urgency over the annual budget cycle and froth over the Compact for Learning reform initiative, the idea of targeting and directing resources to "no point" jurisdictions located in "non metropolitan" areas of the state is an especially hard sell. Anthony Downs put the underlying reason best:

> Public attention rarely remains sharply focused upon any one issue for long...problems suddenly leap into prominence, remain there for a short time, and then, through largely unresolved, gradually fade from the center of public attention.[5]

One such dim area in need of continuous "attention getting" is an region called North Country, a place whose southern boundary is roughly midway across Saratoga and Rensselaer Counties. The same area is bounded by Vermont on the East, Canada(Quebec) to the North and Lake Ontario to the West.

For school reform efforts focused upon "college bound Regents" performance data, the first k-12 districts to appear on the exemplary mapping are at the 3.0-3.5 point consideration of the "close" districts pool. While Lowville district in Lewis county and Madrid-Washington district in St. Lawrence county and Alexandria district in Jefferson county are within the top 200 districts of the entire state, they are not in either the Bulls-Eye or iterations of "close" jurisdictions framing the reform "target."

Be that as it may, the development of Regents oriented change strategies in uncertain times using nebulous meanings of "boundaries" of association may depend upon districts with *any* Regents point count. With this license, I have added the Brittonkill district within Rensselaer county, Town of Webb district in Herkimer county, Keene district in Essex county and North Warren district in Warren county to focus the North Country discussion.

The demonstration of how a *keirtesu* potential network could be mapped within the dim recesses of some regions of the state is only an illustration of what state educators and reform planners could do. There are about forty districts within the North County area that have earned at least one Regents mastery point. Based upon that information alone, a repertoire of phased and systematic involvement can be identified as linking channel options.

It is an Important Discussion So Concede the Reality of Miscommunicating

Those who would build a library of knowledge about the politics of data in the policy process would likely prefer decision making delimited to clear cut situations, particularly with specific observed behaviors of choosing and unambiguous interpretation of results. The dream continues despite the long held appreciation that strict "systems analysis" in public policy making can lead to

> excessive quantification, incapacity to deal with conflicting values, lack of treatment of extra rational decision elements and neglect of problems of political feasibility [6]

The actual influence of information upon any policy process is questioned in two basic ways. First, knowledge may not be used in direct and instrumental fashion to form policies The ongoing flow of organizational events during the school year shape an institutional or corporate accommodation through small, essentially uncoordinated steps. Like sand dunes moving slowly over the Sahara, policy patterns may accrete gradually, often without the direct connection to the formality of a research agenda or even choice maker consciousness.

> Idea fills in the background, supplies the context, from which ideas, concepts and choices derive. Second, ideas are slippery things and even scientists who work in a tradition that requires the citation of sources find it difficult to trace the genealogy of their ideas.[7]

Professor Carol Weiss would argue that research results based primarily on Regents data may be an aid in stimulating discussions, but their actual utility comes from channeling debates over meanings of long term and persistent change of k-12 institutions. Secondary program reform is determined by people becoming convinced of the credibility or legitimacy of a particular reform stance. In emergencies, policies often come into being without the systematic consideration of an explicit issue. They may come from distant memories and explode out of the intellectual history into the contemporary blue.

We find ourselves delimited to the old vaudeville act of "knowing as probing" and "trial ballooning" possible options much of the time. With such nebulousness, we discuss the place holder explanation of the "contemporaneous confluence of choice opportunities" straight faced. [8]

Asserting that we are working with a "dynamic flow" of information, [9] it is assumed that *plausible* rewards and sanctions can be identified and shaped into policy. Further, "chaotic" conditions can be discussed as *potential* parameters for choosing between institutional capacity building for nourishing organizations or three other *possible* ways of investing resources to engage in proactive change.

Hope for stable bases of *predictable* understanding remain despite concessions to the palimpsest created as historic information weaves back into and through "embedded" educational choices. Paradoxically, we continue to appreciate the dual need for identifying both "causally configured sequences"[10] in discussing complex organizations,and simultaneously reaffirming our commitment to an "organic led and managed process of local change" [11]within institutions.

The politicized oxymoron created by just such a crossover does not seem so extreme in the climate of mid-1990's decision making practicalities. For expert system trained policy analysts, however, the knowledge creep of information use within institutionally embedded decision making situations is hard to swallow as an acceptable enigma due to complexity, let alone translate into coherent and grounded discussions about day to day managing.

Being Hard Nosed About it All

Although some continue to be dazzled and amazed by the impact of juxtapositions upon any logical debate, hard nosed analysts demand to know two more handfuls of further clarification. On one hand, if information use disappears when school jurisdictions are described as a "nested hierarchy of closed systems," especially when that organization also creates the imaging of "one best form" of institution,[12] then the relationship between policy and organizing for reform become too "loosely coupled" and "too tenuous" to be of discussion value. [13]

On the other hand, the American system of governing is described as a "marble cake"[14] dynamic understood by tracing historical participation patterns around specific issues within layers of government. If this is true, can we then affirm that large, overarching decisions are "factored" to subunits (or electronic nodes) of the complex organization or does describing actual issue resolution becomes a "dissipate" phenomenon that disappears within the implementing process?[15]

The two questions that demand to to be addressed and the one we should sidestep make this writer's approach another way to concede that opinions of persons of good will differ concerning the core questions of whether *systematic* information about *systemic* change can lead to any directive reform strategies.

Finally, the question no one wants to ask and so will remain in the realm of total mystery for my musings about New York State: When information use is said to disappear because school organization boundaries are defined as "permeable"[16] has politics and organization become one and the same?   If so, even a proactive stance to improve bureaucratic implementation is suspect. We should learn to expect that some policy reform identities may disappear like the sun going behind the clouds, while other understandings become dissolved as an infinite regress of permeable arrangements.

New York City is a District Too Large for State Wide Models

During the 1993-1994 school year there were 285,882 secondary students in New York City. As the City District is approximately 300 square miles, Table 4-1 shows the *secondary grade density* is under 1000 pupils/square mile (for all children the pupil/square mile is 3000+ children).

Table 4-1
The Boroughs of New York City k-12 District, Academic Year 1993-1994

Descriptor	Manhattan	Bronx	Kings	Queens	Richmond
Gr. 9-12 Enrl	55,648	53,526	97,046	65,459	14,203
% White	7.6	6.9	18.5	20.7	65.3
%Afro American	37.3	35.4	49.5	32.6	16.5
%Hispanic	43.8	52.0	24.2	29.6	11.8

Yet, you could look at the same data from a slightly different perspective. The 285,000 children placed in 9-12 grade arrangements of, say, fifty buildings would create site populations of about 5700 pupils per location. That creates a major organization of responsibility and resource distribution in any league of management operations.

Overall, the racial composition of students throughout the entire City finds white students slightly under twenty percent. Afro American and Hispanic students both average over a third of the student body composition city wide. Using racial composition of the k-12 student body as a proxy for dependent variable, the format identified fifteen k-12 districts in the rest of New York State with less than 50 percent white student body. All were located in the City metropolitan area; five in Nassau county, one in Rockland county, six in Suffolk county out on Long Island and three in Westchester county. The island district of Bridgehampton is an obvious anomaly situation; 147 pupils in all grades spread out to a very sparce density and having extremely high valuation assessments of property and personal income wealth.

The other fourteen jurisdictions offer a pool of k-12 districts to begin discusson of the Regents program and the City district. Table 4-2 shows New York City is far better off than Roosevelt, Brentwood, Central Islip and Wyandach districts when the combined wealth ratio indice is used. Jurisdictions considerably better off than the City district in combined wealth ratio are found in East Ramapo, Greenburgh, Port Chester and the Tarrytowns.

In terms of racial and ethnic politics being related directly to the non-white composition of the student body, the fourteen districts with less than half of the students white can be subdivided even further. New York City high schools that are mostly Afro- American could be identified with the Hempstead, Roosevelt and Wyandach jurisdictions. High schools that have a balance between Black and Hispanic students (and more than a fourth white students) could be compared to Freeport and Central Islip districts. City high schools that have a predominant Hispanic minority population could be compared to Brentwood, Port Chester-Rye and Tarrytowns school districts.

Table 4-2
Demographics of Fourteen* k-12 Districts Under 50 Percent White Pupils

District	County	94 Enrl	% Afro	%His	pup/sq mi	CWR
Freeport	Nassau	6408	41	31	877	.88
Hempstead	Nassau	5483	72	26	1520	.86
Malverne	Nassau	2258	51	7	813	1.25
Roosevelt	Nassau	2955	91	8	1856	.46
Uniondale	Nassau	4826	73	17	600	1.33
East Ramapo	Rockland	8701	43	7	277	1.88
Amityville	Suffolk	2929	66	11	570	1.19
Brentwood	Suffolk	12,436	17	35	76	.59
Central Islip	Suffolk	5005	32	34	677	.57
Copiague	Suffolk	3744	33	16	601	.75
Wyandach	Suffolk	2127	91	8	947	.36
Greenburgh	Westchester	1967	52	7	306	2.19
Port Chester	Westchester	3029	16	43	661	1.80
Tarrytowns	Westchester	1822	12	40	589	1.91

* Bridgehampton district in Suffolk County not included

Although there has been some very large problems with missing or incomplete information, the <u>New York: State of Learning</u> document does provide some District of New York City performance statistics for the production of Regents diplomas, college bound expectations and the nine Regents subjects. Table 4-3 shows more than four-fifths of New York City seniors express the intention of "going on to college" but less than one fifth attained the Regents diploma.

Table 4-3
New York City District Regents Secondary Performance, 1991-1994

Subject	1991-92	1992-93	1993-1994
RegDip/ Coll Bd	19/84	21/81	19/79
Global	40/66	40/65	5/63
Hist/Govt	20/73	21/71	23/67
French	5/94	5/93	5/94
Spanish	23/95	23/95	24/95
Interm. Math	29/71	31/68	33/67
Advanced Math	20/81	20/74	22/72
Biology	34/58	33/58	30/63
Chemistry	23/62	22/65	24/69
Physics	13/76	13/72	14/72
Enrollment k-12	950,452	971,690	992,992
% White	19	18	18
% Afro American	38	37	37
% Hispanic	35	36	36

These results make it hard to argue that New York City is simply fashioning a deliberate strategy of substituting Local diplomas for the Regents certificat. It is also clear that the deliberate focus upon racial connotations of organization must then lead back to academic performance and actual test results, no matter how the present debate over the future of compulsory public education turns out over "authentic assessments" and racial re-segregation.

This study seems to suggest that academic monitoring of the City district should focus on Global Studies and let History/ Government off the front burners. Certainly Spanish seems the foreign language of choice for the particular composition of secondary programs throughout New York City.

A good argument could made for monitoring New York City Intermediate Math instead of Advanced Math. However, the whole area of Regents mathematics is about to get fuzzy as variances are approved to count test takers between 50-64 as achieving "minimal competence" thresholds(see next chapter). The State Education Department has invested a great amount of energy in creating an integrated scope of content for the Math 1,2,3 sequence. A key point for continuing the discussion of accumulating course credits for the Regents Biology must be monitored closely too, for this is where the great showdown of the Creationism charge will be determined. Finally, Chemistry should be monitored over Physics due to the condition of New York City secondary education today.

Table 4-4 provides the Regents summary information for the fourteen less than 50 percent white student body districts.

Table 4-4
1993-1994 Regents Performance By Districts With Less than 50% White

District	RD/CB	Global	Spanish	Adv Math	Biology	Chemistry
Freeport	27/88	52/72	42/96	31/75	36/90	15/76
Hempstead	4/71	28/65	17/80	10/38	24/40	10/42
Malverne	24/90	67/67	31/95	24/90	66/74	39/90
Roosevelt	4/82	8/100	1/100	20/9	9/69	12/81
Uniondale	16/81	36/80	39/96	25/86	29/83	28/68
East Ramapo	41/86	55/82	33/98	37/70	47/84	39/81
Amityville	30/68	57/97	20/64	31/63	39/87	34/80
Bridgehampton	35/73	45/100	36/74	27/00	127/64	45/100
Brentwood	29/76	50/81	47/90	31/71	44/91	30/91
Central Islip	21/61	39/73	23/99	22/85	34/93	25/80
Copiague	34/78	43/100	28/91	33/81	68/83	48/86
Wyandach	7/49	42/43	10/70	15/87	24/38	16/25
Greenburgh	36/83	38/98	20/79	38/84	53/88	25/92
Port Chester	23/85	42/88	55/95	41/83	39/74	42/71
Tarrytowns	50/83	56/85	16/100	25/86	51/93	31/64
New York City[17]	19/79	45/63	24/95	22/72	30/63	24/69

•= exemplary point
c = "close" half point

It could be argued that 1993-1994 academic school year is only one-among many. It can also be rationalized that the generally poor performance was due to a rash of "decentralization" indigestion that began before the Ocean Hills-Brownsville mess. The citizens, parents and educators involved daily are the only ones who must live with a judgment based on the accepted *spectrum* of meanings about their children's performance.

Sewanhaka, theDistrict Illustration of a Special Secondary Situation

There are three secondary only or grades 9-12 school districts in New York State. As shown in Table 4-5 below *Sewanhaka would have a ranking of 4.0 and be in the third target iteration* based upon three exemplary threshold points and two one-half point for "close" ranking.

Table 4-5
Regents Course Performance by the Sewanhaka District, 1991-1994

Subject	91-1992	92-1993	93-1994
RegDip/Coll Bd	42/87	42/89	49/88
Global	82/80•	81/79 (c)	78/85 (c)
Hist/Govt	66/74	74/86	73/87
French	8/94	11/99	10/99
Spanish	37/95	41/97•	40/96•
Interm. Math	64/80	61/88	71/83
Advanced Math	52/86	49/90	49/82
Biology	74/80	68/83	69/94
Chemistry	56/85	59/86	55/94
Physics	31/84	34/87	33/91

On the surface Sewanhawa and the other secondary only districts would seem to have automatic crossover to the New York City high schools in policy discussions of Regents program performance by individual clusters of sites. In 1993-1994, Sewanhawa had a student population of 6615, an increase of 7.3 percent in two years. During the same time the white student population declined from 71.1 percent to 56.4 percent.   However, there is the issue of New York City as a fiscal dependent district while the other three 9-12 districts are fiscally independent.

Assuming the fiscal dependent status was insurmountable the possibilities of exploring organizational compatibility between grade k-12 and grade 9-12 structures directly.   Figure 4-2 shows the Sewanhaka district would have the same Regents production point count as eleven other k-12 grade districts throughout the state.

Figure 4-2
K-12 Districts Comparable in Point Count to Sewanhaka

Downstate	Capital	Central	Western
Commack, Suffolk	Chatham, Columbia	Honeoye, Monroe	East Aurora,Erie
Mattituck, Suffolk	Mohawk, Herkimer	Gates Chili, Monroe	Brighton, Monroe
Shorham-Wading, Suffolk	Niskayuna, Schenectady		
Nanuet, Rockland			

We can see (in Table 4-5 on the previous page)that the best features of the Sewanhaka secondary Regents program were found in the Spanish and Global Studies subjects.   Honeoye Falls, Mohawk, Shorham-Wading, Mattituck and Gates Chili districts have also accumulated exemplary or close points in Spanish while Mattituck, Mohawk, Honeoye Falls, Gates Chili and Brighton districts have achieved points in Global Studies.

Extrapolating Change Strategies to a Dim Area of New York

Some nuggets are harder than others to find.   The secondary programs In certain New York districts are so exemplary that they cast a blinding light into the rest of public education in the area.   That light may also be hypnotic because many policy makers cannot seem to look at the full spectrum of meaning of public secondary education for the state.

Yet the educator obligation to every taxpayer is that the child in the most remote, rural environment deserves the same exemplary "college bound" option for life choices as authentically as any other child. Certainly, it will be a different experience from the child in Buffalo or New York City. *These results also suggest that it will not be as enriched as the children in sixty six "target" k-12 districts throughout the state,* but dim regions can be described as making organized efforts toward high quality performance. In the dimmer areas of the state, the policy analyst must become content to play data through multiple iterations of partial points and no points classification to secure an identifiable change network.

To get the first glimpse of the North County we begin with a three district identification in the 3.0-3.5 group of the "close" population. At that level, there three gateway districts on the Lake Ontario side; Lowville of Lewis County, Alexandria district in Jefferson county and Madrid-Washington district of St. Lawrence. The district of Brunswick (also called Brittonkill) in Rensselaer county could provide a "southern" gateway.   The Rensselaer county representation seems necessary to counterbalance the historic tendency of Saratoga county to dominate most policy meanings of information going northward along the Hudson River valley. Certainly, the "target" districts of Burnt Hills and Shendehowa have qualitatively superior Regents secondary programs compared to any district in the entire North Country area.

The policy art work is to approach the secondary improvement process as a "reflected light" relationship with the more advanced Saratoga district while, at the same time, turning up the visibility of Lowville, Alexandria, Madrid-Washington and Brunswick districts.

To create the internal North Country network, the identifying points must be first dropped to the evel. Seventeen districts within the region could begin the rough networking for mutual *keiretsu* exchanges.

> • The Northwest Corner: St. Lawrence/ Jefferson County node: Madrid-Washington district leads two other St. Lawrence districts, Morristown and Potsdam. Alexandria and LaFargeville couple in Jefferson county.

> • The Northeast Corner: Plattsburgh City district holds the fort alone. Suggest consideration of "day trip" arrangements with Tupper Lake in Franklin county.

> • Dead Center in Adirondacks: Long Lake in Hamilton and Keene district in Essex as coordination among the smallest and most remote k-12 jurisdictions in the state.

• Southeast Corner: The Rensselaer district of Brunswick connects to Salem district in Washington County. Salem should then link toward the center of the network with Queensbury in Warren county on one hand and Ticonderoga in Essex county on the other.

• Southwest Corner: From strong programs in Burnt Hills and Shendehowa districts, build upon Saratoga county jurisdictions of Scotia-Glenville and Galway. Town of Webb in Herkimer county and Jefferson district in Schoharie county could be added here.

Twenty seven more districts add to the *potentials* for a North Country networking and change effort. Figure 4-3 lists the group created by the two iterations of identification. There are educators in various other k-12 districts who could have been identified as forming the regional boundary of this mapping venture (eg. Johnstown in Fulton county or Duanesburg in Schenectady county). Districts like Hadley Luzurne could make a reasonable argument for being in another category of grouping for change.

Figure 4-3
Potential North Country/ Adirondack Network of Regents Focused Districts

NW Corner	NE Corner	Middle	SW Corner	SE Corner
Madrid-Washington	Plattsburgh	Long Lake	Burnt Hills	Brunswick
Lowville (Lewis)	Tupper Lake	Keene	Shenendehowa	Salem
Alexandria (Jefferson)			Scotia-Glenville	Queensbury
LaFargeville			Galway	Ticonderoga
Morristown				
Potsdam				
Webb (Herkimer)				
Canton	Chateaugay	Newcomb	Lk. George	Averill Park
Edward-Knox	Beekmantown	Hadley-Lururne	Cambridge	E. Greenbush
Hammond	Saranac	North Warren	Argyle	Ft .Edwards
Ogdenburg(St. Law)		Northville	S. Glens Falls	Granville
Parishville(St. Law)				
Lyme(St. Law)				
Colton-Pierpoint (St. Law)				
Herman-DeKalb(St. Law)				
Copenhagen(Lewis)				
Beaver River(Lewis)				
Genral Brown(Jefferson)				
Carthage (Jefferson)				

The pessimist would continue to note that any North Country network of "college bound Regents programs " is far less exemplary than other collections of New York districts throughout the state. Further, that the proportionate numbers of "non-point" districts in this particular area is also larger than other areas of the state. Another iteration of threshold criteria dropped to the 1.5 -1.0 point identity fills out a Regents networking potential within the North Country.

Communicating About Region and Community as Policy Identities

The lesson for educators to remember when discussing school change that persists over time is that understanding has to be systematically developed. Debate about proper relationships of the jurisdiction as a study of embedded communities is unavoidable. *Proper* is an ambiguous standard in any context, but especially when the public service is compulsory and children of school age must attend some schooling arrangement.[18]

The formal or legal description of the professional obligation raises less concern about proper relationships with community than the more informal social and political meanings of *sufficient and necessary* associations to reach persistent agreements. The difference between the person acting as a professional educator and the educator out of role must be remembered in the spectrum of different meanings about school people influencing community relationships.

Out of the professional role, a teacher or administrator is just the citizen, paying property taxes and, very likely, raising their own school aged children. In my mind, the bureaucratic "civil service" professional is more analogous to the golfing professional who administers a golf course over a long period of time than a teacher, guidance counselor or site administrator actually playing a round of golf .

Three decades ago there was much discussion about generic distinctions between "cosmopolitan" and "local" personalities and the impact upon institutional career paths. In the middle 1990's we must counterbalance the weight of that thinking with the kind of supplemental "portraits"[19] of "good" school administering in different school settings. Under uncertain conditions of proper identification, the personalized ethic of public service will often substitute the organizational counterpart: expectations of Total Quality Management and the ideal of Customer Satisfaction outcomes.

School professionals find the potential for a growing area of miscommunication about what the professional educator does and what school based functions should be. Garrett Hardin[20] wrote about the "tragedy of the commons" that occurred when responsibility for an abstract meaning of public outweighed local or personal identity to a specific task. Using the illustration of cows being herded and grazed on communal assumptions, Hardin argued that the tragedy of ambiguous identity is the creation of a lack of stakeholding or personal ownership where individuals are accountable for their particular cows on grazing lands. The results is the slow erosion of personalized commitments to look after the cowherd as a whole.

Without the personalized connection and sense of mission, the core identity of a network of public and nonprofit service agencies may become preoccupied with the organizational meanings of providing service to "clients" alone. New York State should assume public education will be facing a continuing period of emergency deficit reductions, economic "shortfalls" in revenue estimates and politicized tax cuts for the rest of this century. One immediate efficiency question for public school reform as a statewide investment is whether perpetuating the traditional view of an exemplary Regents secondary programs (successfully or unsucessfully) can co-exist with alternative arguments for investments in "democratic discourse" or new career bound, school-to-work secondary program thinking.

Implications For Data Driven Policy and the Rapidly Approaching 21st Century

Consideration of special conditions within the state wide concerns for improving secondary education would seem to beg for the larger discussions of managerial directives and implementation mandates, especially those that shape rationalizations to act as the original policy expectations about the "why" of reforming.

For the rest of the 1990's an overarching rationale capable of describing systemic change "progress" as a persistent phenomenon seems called for.[21] President Franklin D. Roosevelt's decade of emergency response to the Great Depression was described by Arnold as;

> a situation when the practical measures that Roosevelt was forced to take to relieve distress and get the economy on its feet were in direct violation of the legal theology of the times.[22]

Describing the interface of wholesale government actions operating under massive emergency conditions,Arnold noted that no human institution could possibly follow any consistent or systematic set of principles over long periods of time.

> The detached observer begins with the realization that rational or moral principles are useless as explanations or bases for organizational predictions, but they are of utmost utility in moving groups of people

by social control. the process of absorbing new elements into the leadership *or* policy determining structure remains the key for averting threats to its stability or existence. [23]

To give a pragmatic lesson in how to rationalize conflicting ideals over a five to ten year period,[24] Philip Selznick wrote about the "national agenda" of the Tennessee Valley Authority project and how federal management achieved Institutional persistence through a "cooptive" process.

Whether grassroots organizations were composed of defensive or idealistic individuals, the act of participating absorbed policy variations into the larger national agenda and allowed localized involvement to act as a symbolic proxy for meaningful commitment. [25]

Acting without principles other than "utility" and relying upon "cooptation" to create a spirit of involvement seems a cynical refrom attitude even when crisis is used as justification. Certainly, those efforts to network exemplary secondary programs should continually assess the rationales used for taking collective actions.

"At Riskness" in the Late 1990's

There are two strong supplemental ideas of what "institutional program improvement" might mean for "at risk" child discussions and the late 1990's. One starts with impact on the child as person and "backward maps" to see how original intentions to create a good citizen were adapted to make implementation happen in bureaucratic settings. The results are presented as discrepancies in the form of unrealized goals of the child. The "ward of the court" argument, given when an school child is treated as a "client placement in a stable environment," becomes the organizational justification for the plight of unrealized goals of children.

The second supplement demands pure "envisioning" argument that "at risk" means an endemic condition of all children in public schools. Any loss of organizational capability in institutional processings of "normal" and "central tendency" operations are always concession to the "aggregated" variability of a particular group of human beings (in ages from four to twenty one).

That variability within the "at risk" population makes efforts at consistent policy look like the public school organization simply went to sleep in some case-by-case situations. [26] This uncertainty of the "middle" in New York State could seem a strong reason to consider the horizontal networking between individual k-12 districts that share a common focus upon Regents identity. [27]

Large city school systems are sometimes described as two worlds of "at riskness" within a district environment; the macro world as consumed with continuing economic crisis throughout the public service sector and the micro world as fragmented fiefdoms aligning with their immediate communities for identity and survival. The same argument might be given to large rural areas with many small districts. Most important to this study, is an emerging battleground over definition when the organizational middle focuses upon the adaptive realignments to top and bottom. Finally, insightful discussion of 1960's organizational decentralization, written in response to the political demands for "community representation" and direct "community control," should not be forgotten by those who would internally "devolve" the central offices of the State Education Department into disintegration.

Professor Herbert Kaufman correctly projected that "community control" gains in decentralization, founded upon the representative value of the late 1960's, would likely set the stage for a pendulum swing back toward the centralized expertise and executive driven organization of the late 1970's. [28]   His argument was that the cost to sustaining institutional precedent while increasing community representation of decentralization demands shifts in direct control over the program resources and the direct challenges to classic bureaucractic hierarchy. His laundry list of the dynamic tensions expressed between decentralization and centralization exchanges were;

•politics of decentralization played within the bureaucratic context generates a series of concurrent institutional pressures for dismantling centralization;
• demands for local representation and countervailing demands for centralized executive leadership both increase in volume and,
•ultimately, the needs for neutral or apolitical competence to mediate impasse and logjams in decentralized situation will be heard as an urgent call for expert intervention.

Following the bandwagon of touting general "at risk" condition throughout the 1980's, a hard shift back toward neutrality and expert intervention will not be an easy sell without an era of encouraging the image of being two faced or forked tongue. Some would argue that the confusion generated by Compact for Learning implementation was the "watershed" of such "both-and" pendulum swinging.

For example, when the Board of Regents consolidation and merger efforts were directed toward a special pool of 139 small district jurisdictions in 1991 the political intensity of centralization to decentralization confrontation and realities of "petri dish" policy operations become painfully apparent. The resulting ripple from such a cascade of events into the late 1990's could mean neutral competence may be perceived *less* as a structural derivative of bureaucratic organization and *more* the networked process of expertise exchange established and maintained through technology. [29]

On a happier note, general computer capability and, simultaneously, the internet connection to a "global village" of information access may add new dimensions to thinking about the "one and the many" as simultaneous identifications of horizontal networking occurring in multiple forms.

---

[1] the central tendency or mean score reported may lead to very serious problems in policy interpretation when there is large internal variation in a population under study. For example, a city district with three or more high schools may have very different percentages of children from families below the poverty level or offer very different secondary programs and Regents courses.

Such internal variations are masked when a mean score is sent to the state by such a district.' New York City is only one of many that share this characteristic including a number of the 190 No Point districts with more than 100 pupils per square mile density.   A limitation of this study, or any otherstudy suggesting state wide policy for districts with multiple high schools (including the two high school situations within the thirty three Bulls-Eye districts) must be noted.

[2] Jonathan Kozol argues the natural patterns of racial composition and poverty concentration are *deliberately* reinforced and manipulated by management for the distribution of school resources. Systematic thinking in how to administer "redlined" forms of discrimination are said by Kozol to be reflected by the public school institution. He argues children in city schools, especially the largest systems, have less wealth capability than children in suburbs and that *directly* contributes to lower fiscal effort and educational performance. See Savage Inequalities (New York:)1991

[3] It is a short leap from considering race as a component of community poverty to declaring race as a genetically determined stratification of automatic inferiority. Certainly, the "slippery slope" of that direction is manifest in the "Bell Curve" controversy generated by Charles Murray and S. Herrstein The Bell Curve (New York: Morrow) 1994

For a direct application of such thinking in the older "race/racial" debates I suggest that Harold Cruse, The Crisis of the Negro Intellectual (New York:William Morrow), 1967, leads directly to Michael Novak's The Rise of UnMeltable Ethnics (New York: Macmillian), 1971. For contemporary reflective thinking about City policy in secondary education during the early 1990's, start with David R. Jones, The Urban Agenda (New York: Community Service Society of New York) December, 1994.

4 For general discussion of the policy approaches possible see Charles Bidwell, " Toward Improved Knowledge and Policy in Urban Education" and James Cibulka " Urban Education as a Field of Study" in J. Cibulka (ed) The Politics of Urban Education in the United States (Washington DC: Falmer Press) 1992 , pages 193-200 and 27-44. In the mid-1990's it seems imperative to rekindle Richard Elmore's counsel; " Forward and Backward Mapping: Logics in the Mapping of Public Policy " (ERIC Document 258 011) 1983.

5 Anthony Downs, "Up and Down With Ecology- The 'Issue Attention' Cycle", Public Interest, 29 , 1972, pg. 39. Attention getting may be a generic desire that leads to the strategic consideration of applied politics but it is Murray Edleman, Words that Succeed and Politics that Fail (New York: Academic Press) 1977, that remains most instructive in pondering the "heady rants" of present day New York State politics.

6 Yekehel Dror, " Policy Analysts: A New Professional Service Role in Government" Public Administration Review, 27, 1967, pg. 198 . One of the best discussions of the 1970's planner's craze that followed the heydays of the "policy analysis." The seductive rush of such maelstorm is both applause and Greek tragedy as best expressed by John Friedmann and Barclay Hudson." Knowledge

and Action: Guide to Planning Theory," Journal of the American Institute of Planning (January 1974) pages 1-16

7 Carolyn Weiss, "Knowledge Creep" Organizational Analysis and Development 1980, pg. 385.

8 phrase discussed in Suzanne Estler,"Decision Making" as one of four basic perspectives. Norman Boyan (ed) The Handbook of Research in Educational Administration(New York: Longmans) 1988, Chapter 15.

9 For example, E. Rogers, Diffusion of Innovations (New York: Free Press) 1983

10 For landmark discussion of decision making application see Peter Bachrach and Morton Baratz, "The Two Faces of Power" American Political Science Review. 56, 1962 pages 947-953. Paul Deising, Reason in Society: Five Types of Decisons in their Social Contexts (Urbana: University of Illinois Press) 1962 and Harry Broudy Promise and Paradox (New York: Teachers College Press)l962 should be read in tandem. For the relationship to bureaucracy see P. DiMaggio and William Powell "The Iron Cage Revisited: Isomorphism and Collective Rationality in Organizational Fields" American Sociological Review, 48, 1983, pages 147-160

11 Matthew Miles "What Skills Do Educational 'Change Agents' Need" Curriculum Inquiry 18. 1988, pages 157-193. Also "40 years of Change in Schools" (San Francisco: American Educational Research Association, April, 1992, Division A invitational address.

12 Dimaggio and Powell op cit., David Tyack, The One Best System (New York: Prentice Hall)l974. Also Milbrey McLaughlin " RAND Change Agent Study Revisited Educational Researcher 19, 1991, pages 11-15

13 I deliberately did not cite either Karl Weick or Charles Perrow as a reader check. It is not the Publishing Editors fault. Americans can learn much from studying the Italian struggle to make democracy work. What "too loose" coupling and "too tenuous" means in Italian politics is losing the sense of civic tradition and the strong commitment to see the community persist. Robert Putnam Making Democracy Work (Princeton: Princeton University Press)1993, Many conventional discussion of American educational policy begin with J. Meyer and B. Rowan " The Structure of Educational Organization" in Meyer(ed) Environment and Organizations(San Franscisco: Jossey Bass) pages 78-109

14 Morton Grodzins," The American System" in Daniel Elazar (ed) The American System (Chicago: Rand McNally), 1962. If we cannot somehow get beyond "marble caking" as the end-point to all policy discussion about issue analysis we will remain stuck in this early 1960's benchmark forever. For the raging debate between the organizational structure adherents and the functional view, I say keep the rational choice issue focus on the bench for a quarter or so. see Mark Rushefsky, "Technical Disputes: Why Experts Disagree," Policy Studies Review (May 1983) pages 676-685

15 For the general conceptualization see James March and Herbert Simon,Organizations (New York: Rand McNally) 1958. DiMaggio and Powell op cit. Also Duncan Rae and Michael Taylor " Decision Rules and Policy Outcomes" British Journal of Political Science (January l971) pages 71-90, for an example of the conventional response.

16 Susan Hadden " Symposium on Public Policy Toward Risk" Policy Studies Review May 1982, pages 651-654. Also M. Carley " Political and Bureaucratic Dilemmas in Social Indicators for Policy Making." Social Indicators Research 9, 1981

17 for the past few years Newsday magazine has completed profiles of academic performance for individual high schools and boroughs in the City. The Community Services Center has created an excellent socio-economic data set and has the added advantage of also being disaggregated to the individual school site level for policy analysis.

18 Perhaps the most antimated New York State discussion of such ambiguity is Catherine Cornbleth and Dexter Waugh, The Great Speckled Bird(New York: St. Martin's Press) 1995. Especially Chapter 4 & 5. The legal relationship of in loco parentis (on behalf of the parent) forces the educator into intense introspection and often an uncomfortably intimate proxy role when acting for the benefit of the child in a public school setting.

19 Sara Lightfoot The Good High School (Cambridge: Harvard University Press) 1991

20 Garret Hardin "Tragedy of the Commons" Nature 1981, See Putnam op cit . "Tracing the Roots of Civic Community," pages 121-161

[21] In Chapter 6 we will look at the student foci within ten goals of the Board of Regents and the Statement of Standards by the Bulls-Eye Pittsford Central School District within the context of translating reform expectations.

[22] Thurman Arnold, The Symbols of Government (New York: Basic Books)1935, page 8

[23] ibid pg. 10. Obviously, such an assessment can be viewed as cynical. See Charles Anderson, "The Place of Principles in Policy Analysis" American Political Science Review , 73, September 1979, pages 711-723

[24] Erwin Bettinghaus is one of a whole raft of writers thinking about long held rationalizations. See " Structure and Argument" in Gerald Miller and Thomas Nelson(ed) Perspectives on Argumentation (Chicago: Scott Foresman) 1966 pages 130-155

[25] Phillip Selznick TVA and the Grassroots (New York: Penguin) 1949 page 141

[26] David Cohen and James Spillane "Policy and Practice: The Relations Between Governance and Instruction" in Nina Cobb(ed) The Future of Education (New York: The College Board) 1994, pages 109-156

[27] Michael Kirst and Gail Meister, "The Role of Issue Networks in State Agenda Setting" (Palo Alto: Stanford University Institute on Educational Finance and Governance) 1983. No. 83-A1 Although seriously dated and about California, the Kirst and Meister discussion fits well with the transformation described by Shoshona Zuboff In the Age of the Smart Machine (Cambridge: Harvard University Press), 1984 and RoseBeth Kantor The ChangeMasters (Cambridge: Harvard University Press) 1982

[28] Herbert Kaufman, " Administrative Decentralization and Political Power" Public Administration Review, 29, 1968, pages 3-15

[29] Kirst and Meister op cit.   While the Bulls-Eye and most Target districts seem well connected with technology it is an open question about the present capacity of No Points districts, especially those in "dim" areas of New York State. The new fiefdoms of "issue network" could easily link to BOCES or existing municipal county govenments and help to strengthen the bridging between state level and localized policy concerns. Concerned citizens in New York are probably wondering why little of this has happened.

I suspect the answer is partially found in John Dollard's matrix of understanding class struggle within long standing caste orientations. Although at odds with the "issue specific" behavioral approach, Dollard summed up the cultural context of linkage politics this way, " I see man also as Freud saw him. If Durkheim sees man poised and timeless in the freize of structure, Freud sees him the ambitious beast, shivering in the high wind of culture. Seen close, he smokes." . Class and Caste in a Small Southern Town (New York: Harper & Brothers) 1949, page xiii in Preface.

Chapter Six

Optimistic Expectations But With One Danger

A ground swell of deferred issues accumulated as the chapters progressed. The kind of noise generated by carefully set aside concerns must be listened to and, if you wish any persistent progress within public institutions, respectfully responded to. The Regents tradition is at a crossroads as present conditions promote and denigrate the meaning of Regents secondary programs. This concentrated study of the advanced program structure within school districts does not provide an automatic or definitive justification for continued support of Regents authority.

Strengthening the entire spectrum of secondary programs is critical to New York's educational future. Revitalizing the Regents scope and sequence seems especially necessary in these times because the State of New York *needs the cornerstone of a very steady platform* to rebuild all of public education. The platform must contain the right mix of programmatic and institutional features and the cornerstone must point to its development.

In the sense of trying to save the Regents curriculum and testing program in New York's future, this study does not mean to imply that an alternative network of individual secondary school sites should challenge conventional district jurisdictions. The documented performance in Regents curriculums does not allow a final opinion as to the relative worth of the secondary school versus the middle and elementary schools organization of any particular district. What emphasis on the Regents curriculum does allow is a starting place to frame hard questions about the entire k-12 experience.

For example, can we have excellent Regents productivity in districts with poor middle and elementary school performance? Is it possible to have an exemplary college bound secondary curriculum and an inferior non-college bound program? Is it possible to have an exemplary Regents program that the local community and citizens are disenchanted with? The credibility of the cornerstone argument rests with the answers to such questions. This study identified at least sixty six places to start the process of asking and answering

Assuming the concept of cornerstone can be verified, the public education system of New York has a secure place to develop the larger processes of improvement. Certainly the policy strength of the entire state would be improved by a network of districts with strong Regents programs presented as a most visible evidence of credibility. Such a platform would mute past criticisms claiming severe mistakes in bureaucratic implementation associated with the Compact for Learning. Regardless of the conceptual merits, many citizens remain confused about the meanings of "authentic assessment" and "shared decision making" mechanisms. Regents familiarity helps to regain a sense of public education continuity as well as a strong hedge against the uncertain future. Public education will remain controversial but improvement depends upon losing the preoccupation with looking backward for indictments.

Of course, there is a real danger in assuming that the credibility of institutional strength will be an automatic assurance that educational practice remains excellent. In a conservative era all people concerned with education must be vigilant that the convenience of *stable* institutions (not *static* meanings of curriculum content, instructional practices and administrative governance) do not become a schooling end in its own right. This was a fundamental concern in the early 1950's, the early 1980's and today.

There is a need for appropriate forums to decide the worth of all public institutions that provide compulsory services to "customers" who are mandated to receive service. A network of k-12 districts that share a common identity of exemplary secondary practice seems a good place to start such a forum. Yet, professional educators can no longer talk among themselves. The cloistered nature of the "polite priest craft" is a brand of politics that is decades out of date. The message of the mid 1990's is more involvement of those outside education who can influence and shape public policy. In the late 1990's it will take more than educator concern and initiatives to develop a reform agenda based upon Regents performance.

Two issues must be dealt with. up front First, when the Compact for Learning was announced in 1990 there seemed to be an atmosphere of cultivated deafness among educational professionals. Perhaps it was a form of exhaustion from working to rid the impressions of "nation at risk, " but the mandated implementation of "shared decision making committees," for example, generated few local festivals given in honor of that particular reform initiative. Educators must work hard to overcome the tendency to just "drift" through the late 1990's.

Second, states that have turned "education business" over to Legislators, Executives or corporate interests have not created illustrations of reform panaceas for New York to imitate. Conventional interest grouping create pecking orders of vested interests but most "partnerships" lack long term persistence. Public education improvement is a long haul investment that demands the search for "quick fix" solutions be tempered.

In the end, the issue of basic value of secondary schooling rests with the citizens in general. The cynicism surrounding citizen driven politics today demands the question of forum be addressed beforehand. Just because we can have mass technology capabilities of "town meetings" to create a semblance of citizen sentiment does not justify some new age meaning of forum for deliberation.

The State of New York will be likely in the midst of a Constitutional Convention before the decade is out. Such a Convention would have watershed era implications for re-involving citizens into the core question acting as public decision makers and clarifying the values behind institutional forms of *public s*ervices.

If a Constitutional Convention seems a somewhat Pollyanna suggestion for the legitimate forum of the citizen expression, the pragmatist thinking about what the network of exemplary districts might do together could test the forum idea by wading in the quicksand of diploma versus certificate arguments. Educators have had their shot at defining the expectations for college bound and career bound secondary programs. Except for some abstract concession about the need for a "unitary diploma by the Year 2000" the present day diploma versus certificate debate remains an impasse'. Educators remain unsure about the values citizens feel about high school production so the underlying battleground of particulars continues to document k-12 completion as an uncertain value.

Investments in licensing and certifying particular demonstrations of production more than match the emotions behind Regents versus local diploma debates over the scope and sequencing of curriculum. Enormous egos replace strategies for accommodation. Where did I first hear the phrase, " If the elephants are dancing can the grass help but get trampled?"

It was true that the 1980's "whole village raises the child" sounded pretty vacuous at times transformation to mid 1990's "elephants trampling grass" sounds worse. The Constitutional Convention could either do away with certain elephants or could delimit trampling to grass-free zones. In any case, public education needs such an open airing, especially about the core meanings of productive secondary schools. Hopefully, all of the education institution, from preschool through post secondary, would get center stage in discussions of vital policy investments and what is valued in compulsory services.

For both the forum of *kieretsu* districts and the Constitutional Convention forum, the topic of Regents programs needs top billing. The exemplary Regents performers need to make the very best case possible as the present day cornerstone of a platform serving New York citizens by reinforcing overall institutional stability and by serving the personal interests of high school graduates.

A Time for Optimism

To end on an optimistic note about retaining and improving the Regents authority and curriculum, I would like to offer two arguments for the rest of the 1990's   The first argument is to reaffirm that determining what is good for achieving the Regents goals can translate standards toward concern for student learning at the district level with little effort.   Regents Goals for student performance are broad and flexible enough to use as an interpretative guide for district, school site and classroom operations. The Pittsford Central School District acts as an instructional and institutional illustration of how a local jurisdiction with Bulls-Eye performance transformed a local meaning of concern for student learning .

Pittsford district in Monroe county (near Rochester) offers practical evidence that a local jurisdiction can translate Regents goal expectations into their own strategic implementation of a reforming agenda involving their secondary program. District educators translated student centered Regents Goals into their own student centered Standards of student performance followed, stepping stone-like, through an expression of district Purpose as sets of "umbrellas" (i.e., standards, measures, program and organization) providing eight core indices for systematic monitoring.

But Pittsford surely did not reach that plateau of excellence by delimiting itself to some blind adherence to the Regents as a state level authority.   Pittsford used Regents as an institutional platform of structure and curricular rationale to *blend* with other sources of exemplary expectations about how high school students perform. Pittsford professionals create exemplary curriculum schedules and provide other "peek performance" learning activities due to their participation in a network of high schools sponsored by the Suburban School Superintendent Association.[1]

This blending of high performance expectations and influence may confound the impression of Regents purity inferred by the Bulls-Eye ranking on Regents criteria. *This concession to local translation is crucial to overcome the traditional impression that state level Regents focus must be an exclusive source of curricular authority.*

In the late 1990's other k-12 districts in the state striving for Bulls-Eye excellence can find much organizational value in how Pittsford personnel extended the Regents platform to approach student centered secondary programming. Utilizing a spectrum of exemplary sources (eg. College Board advanced placement courses) helps improve the Regents curriculum when all expectations are focused upon student performance. Districts concerned with "over control by state government" need a source of relief and optimism.

What has been learned about state wide reform in the early 1990's is that promoting extreme decentralization and local autonomy to translate curricular intentions is not, *in itself*, enough to guarantee the chances for honest reform. Needing such optimism for flexibility and local interpretation is critical to get around the pre occupation with state level authority but it does not clean up the policy mess that lets charges of class and caste derail many serious reform discussions before they get started.

The present backlash against the Regents secondary curriculum and testing in New York's *most urban* districts (New York City and districts over 750 pupils per square mile) can not be ignored as an endemic state level condition. The 190 districts that had no Points accumulation in this study included all large and medium sized city districts in the state The continued documentation of exemplary Regents performance by mastery thresholds must expect that a portion of the reading audience associated with urban locations will judge efforts at such documentation as "racist work" and sneer with curled lips[2] at the recommendation for leading New York's next wave of reform with a network of local k-12 districts that are basically suburban, rich and populated with white students .

Similarly, it would not be surprising to find a knee-jerk backlash response to the "Japanese thing for reform," as former President Bush might say. While not racial in the big city politics sense, a sigh of relief about achieving an improved "Regents thing" will only come if Japanese vertical and horizontal networking advice can be identified as borrowing from American demonstrated initiatives.

Either of the above speculations sound like an ethnocentric attitude with ugly, politically incorrect, overtones that should be avoided at all costs in a pluralistic and democratic society. But optimism for another wave of conscious improvement of secondary education rests with honest concession to what side tracked much of the Regents Action Plan and Compact for Learning initiatives.

Because of the past fifteen years, I feel perceptions of racism and jingoism must be extracted from where they are buried within the technicalities of systemic reform strategies or surrounding the dangerous tendencies to unravel New York performance accountability (such as variance policy blurring mastery and minimal expectations for learning).

To set the stage for involving those who must have critical discussions about what is racist and jingoistic, there seems a need for an American demonstrated supplement to the *keiretsu* rationales for networking. I suspect most New Yorkers will like the undertone of the supplemental American argument very much, for the historical layers of accumulated investments in education and economic development in regions around the state are its centerpiece.

The second argument for optimism about reform during the rest of the 1990's decade is about the existence of *critical resources to improve already in place*. Existing concentrations of talent, strategy and once highly active resource pools contain a naturally occurring *dynamic* generating reform opportunities and resembling spontaneous combustion. For those Americans that must temper foreign leadership by the Japanese (or any other country,) the second argument for optimism comes from understanding what has happened in Silicon Valley, California.

In short, the Silicon Valley situation suggests that areas where resources are already concentrated in layers and clusters of previous investment contain natural ebbs and floods of new opportunities for change occurring all the time. These concentrations of enrichment have opportunities for regional resurgence options that occur despite structures and institutions that suggest a static or dying condition.

While most resurgence tendencies go unnoticed beneath a threshold needed for recognition, some are strong enough to break through and create unexpected change activities. The Silicon Valley concentration of resources that revitalized that area due to an unexpected surge within existing arrangements resembles numerous locations throughout New York that are presently bubbling with similar resurgent tendencies.

Politics is sometimes about blanketing and deliberately ignoring possibilities for changing. Politics is sometimes about robbing from one group of needy to redistribute their scarce resources to another grouping of needy or not so needy As the 1990's noose of economic downturn tightened upon New York, the state became notorious for exhibiting episodes of such suppression and "geographic patronage." The impression is given to those anticipating the need for another large scale improvement of secondary education throughout New York is that , other than playing musical chairs with shrinking options and cannibalizing each other, regions have lost the ability to consider their resurgence possibilities.

The history of New York leading to the mid 1990's has become the perceived enemy of thinking future reforms. It is *as if* the history that identified New York among the leaders in the country and country for such a long time is now the reason many policies for reforming are rationalized as incapable of working in particular locations. The contemporary status quo that represents the accumulated resources for the past three centuries is not presented as a resource base of potential resurgence but the reason new things do not get done.

Yet, there has never been a policy world of accumulated resources, capabilities for organizing and new forms of connecting such as the one we New Yorkers experience every day. The experience in Silicon Valley suggesting the idea of spontaneous resurgence seems plausible enough consider strategies for acknowledging that particular feasts can occur amidst general famine conditions. Once conceded, even the most unlikely k-12 arrangements to find dramatic improvement could be imagined as enjoying episodes "blips" of rich opportunities. [3]

In other words, there are reasons for optimism in thinking about educating during the rest of the 1990's if we had concrete examples that spontaneous resurgence are more than pipe dreams. Silicon Valley went from stale, cannibalized and disheartened area of California to a revitalized region with a resurgence that took peculiar twists New Yorkers can appreciate. An optimistic argument must also lead toward further value considerations of what makes reform persist. For example, those concerned with the relationship of educating to economic vitality must address the difficult question of whether advanced curriculums and "college bound" expectations are related student employability and a persistent improvement in the contributions educated pupils make within the job structure.

Parents cannot look their children in the eyes and say that the diploma or certificate are only "union cards" or "tickets" into an educator sanctioned exclusive club. Thinking like that makes the present a dangerous time. In the grand sweep of trying to reform secondary education it is often the small, incremental adjustments that contain the core ingredients of what the organized system of schooling is really about. We must appreciate the "sunk cost" details that will govern and channel opportunities for making changes as much as waiting for the resources and opportunities to revitalize the on going situation. There are reasons for sensing danger .

One such "sunk cost" danger question that can be worked on now is the blurring of minimal and mastery thresholds in accounting for student performance in Regents subjects.. As a political response to the rapidly increasing stratification in our society a variance intending to blur is understandable , but the" 50/64" variance approved for secondary programs in History/Global Studies, Biology and Math 1,2 & 3 sequence remains a *perverse* variance for the issue of actually accounting for student performance.

The danger to thinking about reform is when this variance is lumped in with others approved in the name of increasing local autonomy, for it is very different from the conventional meanings of variance granted for curriculum experimentation. It should be abolished.

Translating Regents Goals Into Local District Reform Expressions

Of course, the cornerstone of the Compact for Learning or any other progressive reform initiative depends upon the State Education Department's promotion of flexibility and local discretion in making curricular decisions. The student or pupil learning is the final rationale underlying both Regents and local authority to educate.

The Board of Regents Goals for Education in the Elementary, Middle and Secondary Students guarantee the necessary abstraction of expressed purpose in helping students to allow local discretion. The Goals have developed throughout the 1980's and 1990's and represent a comprehensive statement of formal intentions. Figure 5-1 lists the general goals and subgoals that rationalize curriculum decision making throughout all of New York State public education.

Figure 5-1
Select Regents Goals for Elementary, Middle and Secondary Students

Goal 1: Each student will _master_ communication and computation skills as a foundation to;
1:1 think logically and creatively
1:2 apply reasoning skills to issues and problems
1:3 comprehend written, spoken and visual presentations
1:4 speak, listen to, read and write clearly and effectively in English
1:5 perform basic mathematical calculations.*
Goal 2: Each student will be able to apply methods of inquiry and knowledge learned through the following disciplines and use the methods and knowledge in _interdisciplinary_ applications;
2:1 English language arts
2:2 science, mathematics and technology
2:3 history and social science
2.4 arts and humanities
2.5 language and literature in at least one language other than English
2.6 technical and occupational studies
2.7 physical education, health and home economics
Goal 3: Each student will acquire knowledge, understanding and appreciation of the artistic, cultural and intellectual accomplishments of civilization.
Goal 4: Each student will acquire and be able to apply knowledge about political, economic and social institutions and procedures in this country and other countries.
Goal 5: Each student will respect and practice basic civic values and acquire and use those skills, knowledge, understanding and attitudes necessary to participate in democratic self-government.
Goal 6: Each student will develop the ability to understand, appreciate and cooperate with people of different race, sex, ability, cultural heritage, national origin, religion, and political, economic and social background, and to understand and appreciate their values, beliefs and attitudes.
Goal 7: Each student will acquire the knowledge of the ecological consequences of choices in the use of the environment and natural resources.
Goal 8: Each student will be prepared to enter upon post-secondary education _and/or_ career level employment at graduation from high school.
Goal 9: Each student will develop knowledge, skills and attitudes which will enhance personal life management, promote positive parenting skills, and will enable functioning effectively in a democratic society.
Goal 10: Each student will develop a commitment to life long learning and constructive use of such learning , with the capacity for undertaking new studies, synthesizing new knowledge and experience with the known, refining the ability to judge and applying skills needed to take ethical advantage of technological advances.

*= several other subgoals are listed but not relevant to this discussion

Each k-12 district is allowed to innovate and adapt their secondary program to the perceptions about local needs and conditions. Regents Goal Three reflects expectations for promoting the arts, Goal Five for civic values, Goal Seven for nourishing ecology and Goal Nine as personal life management. Each goal seems to belong as "local discretion" decisions and beyond the deliberative strategies of state level reform agendas. These are the heart of local interests and have centered controversies that simply dissolved state wide networking efforts in the past.

The Pittsford Example of Interpreting Student Focus

Pittsford Central School District has a simple and effective way to translate Regents goal expectations into standards of performance for their students. Figure 5-2 lists the eleven Pittsford standards.

Figure 5-2
Pittsford Standards of Performance for Students

Students will demonstrate the ability to;
1. understand and apply knowledge of liberal arts, fine arts, mathematics, the sciences and mental and physical wellness.
2. use critical thinking skills and decision making to solve problems.
3. communicate effectively in both oral and written expression.
4. communicate in a second language.
5. evaluate and deal effectively with personal strengths and weaknesses.
6. maintain the highest possible ethical standards.
7. develop a commitment to lifelong learning.
8. cooperate and communicate with others.
9. accept and appreciate a multicultural community.
10. be sensitive to individual differences and respect others.
11. develop a responsibility to the local/global community.

Figure 5-3 presents a schematic illustration of the systematic relationship between standards of student performance (e.g., the purpose of providing secondary instruction), traditions of the district and trends in reform activities.

Figure 5-3

The Pittsford Plan for Perceptual Coherence in Standards Thinking[4]

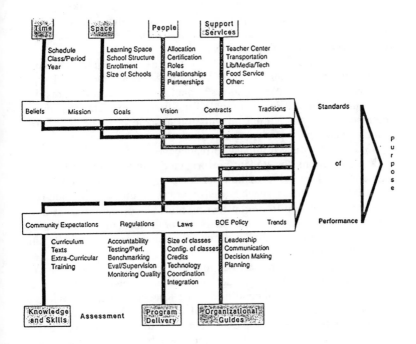

Pittsford district assumes teams will translate standards of student performance into curricular and organizational expectations. An "umbrella" arrangement is envisioned for teams to identify the outcomes(the what) and methods (the how) in helping students meet standards.

Standards of performance provide the umbrella for consideration of measures of performance. Measures act as an umbrella for actual program decisions and, in turn, program acts an umbrella for organization within the district. The actual process of translating "umbrellas" assumes eight core dimensions in making and implementing educational policy. The eight dimensions are time, space, people, support services, knowledge and skill, assessment, program delivery and organizational guides.

Teams within Pittsford use these dimensions to guide thinking about both traditions and trends. What will contribute most to a happy face reaction among New Yorkers is the fact that a local k-12 district can translate broad Regents Goals for Students expectations into a sequence of organizational information capable of strategic reform planning about pupil performance.

What will concern the astute reader the most is whether district wide expectations for student performance can be further refined to expectations for the secondary school programs. For example, in considering facilities space the size of an elementary school is a different proposition from considering high school size. Community expectations for extra-curricular activities or the meaning of monitoring quality as a school trend also differ between elementary, middle and secondary education.

In sum, the schematic in Figure 5-3 rationalized a pipeline of crucial deliberations but actual decision making demands knowledge of particular organizational conditions. The Regents program provides a platform to reference the what and how of delivering a quality secondary experience. Local educators and citizens are not required to like or agree with the Regents approach but counter points and alternative arguments should reference to the existing Regents arrangement.

Another Argument for Optimism: The   California Illustration of Regional Resurgence

Although on the other coast, many New Yorkers identify strongly with California as a collection of "bright" concentrations due to previous resource investments. One such spot, perhaps the brightest, is

Silicon Valley.   Economic resurgence is happening there because of
the pool of American creative talent, professional expertise and
infrastructure of businesses already concentrated and available.   The
California bright spot resurgence does not depend upon that state's
ability to borrow from the demonstrated magic of Japan. It depends
upon the existing concentration of talent and resources *reigniting* into
new economic resurgence.

If the ideas of availability and capability are supposed to guide
strategic calculation, then there are patterns of concentration and
dispersion expressing themselves all the time.   An American based
economic analogy could set the stage for educators considering the
relation of academic reforming in New York State and an expanded
meaning of resurgent as bright spot secondary programs.

The hope for convincing New Yorkers to be optimistic about the
future rests with a *keiretsu-like* networking occurring in California's
Silicon Valley. What Silicon Valley represents to California can be
argued as existing and potentially available in many areas throughout
New York State, especially where Bulls-Eye and Target districts are
found.   Based upon previous economic investment, New Yorkers can
imagine the potential regional resurgence in the Binghamton-Corning
area, metropolitan Rochester, Syracuse, the Capital District area or the
Dutchess and Orange county region as easily as Westchester, Nassau
and Suffolk counties.

But the seeming elitism inherent in translating an assertion of such
concentration is much more than the obvious fact that schools in
wealthy communities afford the "pricey" Regents secondary curriculum
easier than New York districts in poor community settings.   The
horizontal networks within the California region are now creating an
economic resurgence built upon existing pools of creative talent and
professional expertise mixed with the infrastructure of businesses
already concentrated in that area. If the concentration of talent and
infrastructure available for economic resurgence is in the same ballpark
of sociological reality that k-12 districts with exemplary secondary
programs can embed as community relationships, then chances for
networking through Regents programs are improved.

The hope for sustained and systemic change occurring throughout
the state begins with the extension of the present concentrations of
exemplary educational achievement behaviors occurring in
communities with the most *plausible* description of regional
resurgence. New York State has a long and strong tradition of
exchanging policy identities with California, Pennsylvania, New Jersey,
Massachusetts and Vermont.   Among the pecking order elite

Californians from Silicon Valley may only acknowledge their Massachusetts "Route 128" counterparts as kindred spirits, yet many New Yorkers in Rochester (Kodak), Schenectady (General Electric), Dutchess and Ulster counties (International Business Machine) or the Capital region (Albany state government) can certainly appreciate what possible resurgence might mean for local economics and education alike.

In 1990 AnnaLee Saxenian[5] explained that the resurgence of the Silicon Valley could *not* be explained by focusing upon either the neo-classical vision of competitive markets and individual firms reproducing by increased entrepreneurship. Similarly, neither could resurgence be explained by the national policy advocates claiming government support and consolidation of key technology sectors. Instead, she argued,

> The resilience of the Silicon Valley economy is the product of the region's dense network of social, professional and commercial relationships...best viewed as an American variant of the industrial districts in Europe-technologically dynamic regional economies in which networks of specialist producers both compete and cooperate in response to fast changing global markets.....*the region, not the firm, is the locus of production.* The result is a decentralized system which is more flexible than the traditionally vertically integrated corporation.(emphasis added) [6]

Some New Yorkers may be as unimpressed with California using a European reference[7] to discuss regional resurgence as the suggestion of an American alternative to horizontal *keiretsu.* However, the evolution of Silicon Valley that created the dense social network potentials of today do have an immediate and concrete relationship to New York in the mid 1990's. Professor Saxenian notes;

> Ironically, the region's established producers that helped to create the infrastructure during the 1950's and 1960's abandoned it during the 1970's as they shifted to high volume production. *They came to view regional traditions of information sharing and networking as signs of immaturity rather than sources of dynamism,* and they distanced themselves from customers and suppliers as they standardized products and processes. The 1980's start ups, by contrast, are formalizing collaborative relationships with customers and suppliers, both within and outside the region.(emphasis added)[8]

Intel Corporation, for example, promoted the "market pre-fabricated mass produced solutions to users."[9]   Unfortunately, many New York businesses and school districts in the areas with the most potential for regional resurgence still operate with a similar 1970's style of non collaboration and an *autarkic* approach to mass production.

With an autarkic approach the firm (or district) standardizes products and processes to achieve high-volume output and to move down the "learning curve." The autarkic firm sees little need for the ongoing interaction with customers, suppliers and competitors that characterizes specialty production. In California's Silicon Valley the shift to high volume production by autarkic firms was coupled with efforts to hedge against business cycles by double ordering from suppliers during boom times and abruptly canceling orders during downturns. Finally, driven by pressures of commodity production to minimize costs, the autarkic firms shifted manufacturing out of the region to lower cost locations across the United States and overseas.

As the 1980's began, it seemed that only high level research, design and prototype production would remain in high cost Silicon Valley. Although active management could overcome some of the problems in spatial separation of design, manufacturing and assembly, the victim in persistent economic vitality seemed to be in the growing gulf between design and manufacturing.

How did Californians use the dense social networks and local institutions to foster the recombination of experience, skill and technology into new, revitalized enterprises?

> It is not simply the concentration of skilled labor, suppliers and information that distinguish the region (as traditional economic accounts would have it). A variety of regional institutions- including universities, several trade associations and local business organizations and a myriad of specialized consulting, market research, public relations and venture capital firms- provide technical, financial and networking services which the region's enterprises cannot afford individually. *By socializing costs and risks and pooling technical expertise*, these institutions allow Silicon Valley's specialist firms to continue to innovate and react flexibly.(emphasis added)[10]

Again the implication for economic resurgence rests with a new state of mind that the original autarkic firms in the region refused to adopt. Economic resurgence is the result of a social movement and socializing phenomenon that helped reproduce a "sense of community." The attention to a collection of individuals operating as a social network within a region explains the operating meaning of community.

Unlike the implicit underpinning of Asian harmony that governs the collective bonding within horizontal *keiretsu*, the Silicon Valley version of social density and exchange has a more American version of sharing and collaborating among individuals.

> *A shared commitment to advancing technology-derived originally from the common formative and professional experiences of engineers in the region-* transcends inter-firm rivalries.   The networks of association defy sectored barriers: individuals move easily from semiconductor to disk drive firms or from computer to network makers.   They continue to meet at trade shows, industry conferences and seminars. In these forums, relationships are easily formed and maintained, technical and market information is exchanged, business contacts are established and new enterprises are conceived. (emphasis added)[11]

Can New York State educators in regions with high concentrations of Bulls-Eye and Target districts find the same sense of loyalty and shared commitment to educational excellence in secondary education? Can the intellectual property created by an outstanding Regents college bound program in one district evolve into a general status for improving and unifying a number of districts as they network in different areas of the state?

> This is not to suggest that conflicts are absent in Silicon Valley. It is the very intensity of competition among local producers that spurs the technological innovation for which the region is famous. *In fact, competitive rivalries often become highly personalized, as status is defined by technical excellence and innovation as much as by market share.* Lawsuits and conflicts over intellectual property are now commonplace. Yet even as these competitive pressures intensify, the sense of loyalty and shared commitment to technological excellence unifies the members of the industrial community.(emphasis added) [12]

Certainly, the exemplary performances documented in this study when coupled to the Compact for Learning era of decentralized reform suggest the potential.   There remains, however, the danger of monopolistic thinking. Consortiums consisting of a number of Bulls-Eye, target and "no point" districts seem to be the desired regional network, but such arrangement run the danger of domination or exclusion by the best.

Professor Saxenian notes the dangers of the Sematech consortium to full regional development in Silicon Valley and New Yorkers remember what General Electric, International Business Machines and

Kodak meant when they discussed "sharing" and "collaborative development" before down sizing or trying to move out of the state. It is clear that the conventional thinking of New York economic development has been that large, established firms dominate the market and thinking about change to new directions.

> Sematech, the semiconductor manufacturing consortium, has limited promise as an industrial strategy because its membership is severely limited. Only fourteen of nearly three hundred semiconductor producers in the United States are members of Sematech and *none of Silicon Valley's recent start ups have joined the consortium because its prohibitive fees exclude all but the largest firms.* While carefully designed joint research projects could help preserve the technological position of the United States semiconductor industry, a program which excludes so many of the industry's most innovative producers is unlikely to do so.(emphasis added) [13]

Finally, The Danger

Most public expressions of State Education Department retreat are found in the strong challenges to state approved syllabi, subject centered curricula and year end administration of state testing. Yet, by far, the greatest danger to thinking about advanced, college bound secondary programs is the blurring of mastery thresholds of performance with minimal expectations to graduate from high school.

There is no immediate reason why New York k-12 jurisdictions cannot have clear standards and expectations for both minimal achievement and mastery achievement. For years the Regents Competency Test (hereafter RCT) has had its own testing format and standards for adequate performance. The danger occurs when minimal expectations are "beefed up" to stand in as a temporary proxy for actual mastery performance or, more to my immediate concern, when mastery standards for "passing" Regents course examinations are adjusted downward.

The reason given for such downward dilution is never academic or intellectual in a policy active way. The *organizational* scope and sequencing of secondary program curricula designed to help the *institution* operate may actually be facilitated by blurring minimal threshold and mastery expectation of effort. Regents slides easier on the way down, but whether the slide is fruitful in terms of learning anything except how to go fast is a real question.

Those that believe there is no danger (i.e., the authority of Regents will compensate for any institutional failing at classification or

implementation) will already object to the initial elimination of
Comprehensive English, Basic Mathematics and Global Studies as
Regents subject areas . Such delimitation as a researcher watching
New York State for the past five years was an easy choice. So many
New York State k-12 jurisdictions have transformed the strict
intentions of the original advanced Regents curricula in these three
subjects that they are virtually useless for any state level policy on
beginning courses toward an advanced curriculum path.

The assessment of Regents secondary subjects in this study were
limited to nine courses that felt comfortable when thinking about
advanced college bound curricula in the mid 1990's. This limiting is
similar to arguing the k-12 district population as 649 units for analysis
because of the bureaucratic reality of grade structure. The 649 districts
do not create exactly the same meaning of state wide educational
system as either the 718 jurisdictions cited in New York: State of
Learning (for 1993-1994) or the 694 district population preferred by the
New York State Education Department purist (population of
jurisdictions based upon at least eight full time equivalent staff).

At present, the danger of blurred meaning is focused upon to the
Regents subjects of History/ Government, Biology and Intermediate/
Advanced Regents Mathematics. The potential disaster to longitudinal
study of Regents performance is the State Education Department
approved "variances" that allow a modification to the "successful
passing as 65" mastery standard in these subjects. Appendix K lists k-
12 districts that received approved "50-64" variances between January
1994 and June 1995. Other districts are likely to have received the
approved 50/64 variance since that time.

It is my feeling that the widespread use of year end Regents testing
used to identify subgroups of students scoring between 50 and 64 as
successfully passing the minimal competency requirement (RCT) to
graduate from high school will also confound all substantive state wide
evaluations of Regents mastery in these subjects. If one objective
cannot be accomplished without the expense to the other then the
successful completion option should be stopped.

Of course, the cornerstone of the Compact for Learning or any other
progressive reform initiative depends upon State Education Department
promotion of flexibility and local discretion in making curricular
decisions. Each k-12 district must be allowed to innovate and adapt
their secondary program to local needs and conditions. Professor Linda
Darling-Hammond becomes quite impassioned in her assertion that
local educators and citizens must struggle for determination of their
local secondary program and that grassroots struggle must be free of

state level mandates. The State Education Department oversight role is seen as much the enemy of progressive reform and the approved syllabi, subject centered, end-of-year testing meanings of curriculum are weapons of oppression.

As questionable as that kind of argument is in promoting more than a polemical bridge to state level "frameworks" for curriculum or in justifying portfolios as assessment devices developed by "authentic" local participation, it does not lead to what seems are dangerous kinds of variances. The danger variance is one that argues that year end Regents test results can evaluated against a minimal expectation for a part of the students taking a course, as opposed to a mastery threshold for successful completion of the subject.

The danger variance identifies the group of student test takers scoring between 50 and 64 as "passing" the minimal competence requirement in select Regents subjects. The students do not register on state level records as being unsuccessful or failing the Regents subject in the course they attended for a full semester or year. The New York State Educational Department approved hundreds of such variances on the grounds that these students were to be now classified with those passing the Regents Competence Test (RCT) of minimal performance expectations.

During the 1994-1995 year January 1994 through June 1995 several hundred k-12 jurisdictions applied and received the approval to count students this way. The reader who has participated in a successful whale watch off the Eastern seaboard or West coast knows the sensation of watching the flip of the great tail and disappearance of a massive mammal. It is hard to believe that the tons of animal so visible one moment are suddenly gone and its new location is somewhere below out of sight. This is the sensation of monitoring the numbers of New York school districts that applied for and received approval to adjust the meaning of "successfully passing" the year end test in the Regents subjects of History, Government, Biology and the Intermediate/Advanced Mathematics sequence.

Policy analysts must understand that the variance concern of being "out of the loop" in annual state reporting of academic performance for up to three years is not the same as the shifting of students to RCT identification. The state level issue of reporting official and useful policy information to legislators and citizens in Academic Year 1995-1996 and beyond remains paramount.

There is an effect of such variance approvals upon samples identified as (a) those pupils who stayed in a particular class all year and decided to take the year end test, (b) those who scored between 55-

64 and, because of the variance, are now counted in the group successful in meeting the Regents minimal performance threshold and (c) the cohort of successful passing Regents test students in the subjects under question.   Certainly the combined effects of such alteration confounds any single meaning of advanced secondary curriculum subject associated with the Regents name.

In one year one hundred and seventy two (26% of model) New York districts received approved variances in Regents History/ Government, one hundred and twelve (17%) jurisdictions received approved variances in Regents Biology and forty six(7%) districts received approved variances in the Regents Intermediate/Advanced Mathematics subjects [see Appendix K for individual districts]. In each case, the variance was approved to count the students scoring between 50 and 64 as passing the Regents Competency Test for minimal performance of all New York secondary students rather than failing the Regents "college bound, advanced" curriculum subject.

While a handful of these districts in each academic subject were Bulls-Eye, the vast majority were "no points" districts that did not qualify for the target analogy. In other words, the danger of modifying the *mastery* meaning of "65 successful passing" to improve *minimal* competency threshold results with more pupils "passing" is that the variance approvals were given to many districts with mediocre secondary program performances between 1990 and 1994.

Thoughts for the Next Reading

Some reformers may be disappointed with the seemingly status quo assumptions throughout this text. Retaining the Regents authority and secondary program legacy as a platform for both late 1990's improvement efforts and present day institutional and curricular stability in New York is conservative.   Some may find my warning of the dangers in blurring mastery and minimal thresholds of academic performance downright obstinate and reactionary.   Certainly, this final chapter counseling optimism simply because k-12 districts are capable of transforming Regents intentions into local meanings or because regional concentrations of talent and resources have a potential for spontaneous revitalization can be misinterpreted as escapist.

I can only respond that sticking to the details found in the information about secondary performance studied and recommending a rebuilding agenda for New York's public education built on the backs of the highest performing k-12 districts is pragmatic.

A careful reading of the footnotes in this and previous chapters will make clear that simple reliance upon the conventional (and often intellectually preferred) approach of asserting first principles or moral premises may lead to Yeat's conclusion that "the centre cannot hold." The institutional turmoil that has resulted from the wild pendulum swings of organized reversals when reforming by top down, ratchet down strategies then in reforming by bottom up, bubble up made me suggest that New York should consider Italian politics as its model of continuity, commitment and community. Reforming to achieve high performance in the late 1990's must embrace the pragmatics of institutional context, not praying fervently for reality to wither away in the face of philosophic pronouncement.

Similarly, New Yorkers can deal with the racial and ethnic implications of democracy and pluralism values, but only by recognizing that the "pandaemonium" Daniel Moynihan describes in the socio-political context of Bosnia and Serbia are differences of degree (not kind) of political expression evident in New York State.

Like the Balkan states, New York educational reform could lose its "wiggle room" for mediation of what the public organization means in practical terms as the public's school. Zero-sum thinking about the idea of high performing secondary settings could grow to dominate a culture of accommodation for resistance to those desiring war over peace. One only has to read the viciousness of charge and counter charge leveled over The Great Speckled Bird argument[14] (concerning the development of curriculum frameworks in California and New York) to get an indication of the "centre cannot hold" in conventional academic discussions today.

Bill Honig, Catherine Cornbleth and Dexter Waugh are not mincing words or splitting hairs about neo-nativist, assimilationist or racist charges against one another. The irony that drips from their mean-spirited exchange is hinted in the lofty interpretations about curricular frameworks and "identity" that

> weave strands of knowledge and cultural understanding, democratic understandings and civic values, skill attainment and social participation. True patriotism celebrates the moral force of the American idea as a nation that unites as one people the descendants of many cultures, races, religions and ethnic groups.[15]

The devil rests in the details, and the road to intellectual hell is paved with arguing abstract intentions. Call me conservative or over cautious, but I argue for future networking of exemplary districts built upon improving the existing Regents legacy as a deliberate hedge to the present climate of hypocrisy.

Yet, there also seems an obligation to end this text by reemphasizing two critical issues that future horizontal networking efforts would face whether those involved wish it or not. Information can only set the stage for beginning the political consideration of such issues.

In Chapter Five the swamp of possible miscommunication and logic traps were listed as problems of meshing special district situations within general state wide policy for Regents curriculum Down state New York will remain two policy worlds for secondary program improvement; Bulls-Eye and target districts on one hand and New York City and No Points districts with more than 750 pupils per square mile on the other.

Second, in Chapter One, the question of equity was addressed with an underdeveloped country application. For a state wide study like this, the resource investment strategy for underdeveloped countries could easily be suggested as a proxy for distribution (and redistribution) of resources to reform academically underdeveloped districts. But are the educationally "dim" areas of New York State equivalent to an underdeveloped nation's economic status when we start deliberating over "capacity building" in strategic reform efforts? Can an honest analogy between countries of the globe and districts of the state be made?

The entire argument for mobilizing the best developed districts into a common network of exemplary performers *may or may not* include the corollary reform agenda to ultimately help the "dim" or underdeveloped parts of New York's academic world. In New York State, the fully developed Bulls-Eye jurisdictions and the ones striving enough to be in the exemplary Target districts are approximately ten percent of all k-12 districts in the model. Should they determine reform initiatives and "seed" investments state wide or would it be more equitable to specify direct funding for all No Points districts as an undifferentiated, blanket investment? Could the latter policy option be justified as serving the "marginalized populations" of academic "underdevelopment?"

It may be that the key to equitable choice decisions by a network of k-12 districts rests with the four hundred and thirty four "some" Points jurisdictions described in Chapter Four. This seems the only group that could possibly negotiate a meaning of equity in a direct elite and non elite contest for control of reform direction. Such mediation would either be an expression of positive commitment toward Regents excellence or a reflection of confusion and uncertain feelings due to a lack of authentic Regents embedding through all districts. In either case, the political culture of the Regents as a New York State curricular phenomenon would be decided as an operating network of districts.

---

[1] Pittsford District is an active member of the Suburban School Superintendents Association. A recent survey conducted by the Pittsford district listed the high school schedules of networking high schools throughout the nation: The Palo Alto, Claremont and Redwood school districts in California, the New Trier, Rich Central, Lake Forest, Hinsdale Central and Highland Park school districts in Illinois, the Grosse Point and Bloomfield Hills districts in Michigan, the North Allegheny and Conestoga high schools in Pennsylvania, the Westfield and Scotch Plains-Fanwood districts in New Jersey, the Needham high school in Massachusetts, the Edina school district in Minnesota. Three other associated New York State high schools (besides Pittsford) are Sutherland, Mendon and Scarsdale high schools. The reader might remember that Scarsdale is one of eleven districts that produce less than ten percent Regents graduates but have more than ninety percent of seniors intending to go on to college.

[2] We must make the clear distinction about the raw race and ethnic politics that trigger "the fire next time" promises as white against black, black against Korean, Latino against white and infinite other combinations as vested interest play off one another. This is Madison's "venal character" run amok as 1990's check and balance structures crumble and fail to contain contemporary mobilizations. The true nature of lip curling will likely come from the state level version of what Fukuyama calls international "hyper realists," those that "believe that international life is a relentless, amoral clash of national interests and that America should be guided by mere balance-of-power considerations." The anger expressed by Cornbeth and others about the Regents approach to reforming social studies and history curriculums in the late 1980's echoes the anger expressed by Moynihan as he concludes America policy seems incapable of conceptualizing a world where states break up and where the intellectual challenge is to *"make a world safe for and from ethnicity,* safe for just those differences which large assemblies, democratic or otherwise, will typically attempt to suppress." See Francis Fukuyama, " The Beginnings of Foreign Policy" The New Republic, August 17, 24, 1992, page 24, Catherine Cornbeth et. al., The Great Speckled Bird (New York: St. Martin's Press, 1994 pages 17-20, 74-87 and Daniel Patrick Moynihan Pandaemonium Cambridge: Oxford University press, 1993, pages 165-170, 173-174.

[3] Again, this study track was seven years for Regents diploma percentages and three years for Regents course evaluations in nine subjects. If I understand the Silicon experience, it is about a region that was the premier place in the nation in the 1960's and 1970's, then went from boom to bust in the 1980's and finally kick started itself in the early 1990's. The author of the Silicon story makes the resurgence sound like the antithesis of systematic planning and more like catching the updraft of an unexpected explosion of surplus and too compressed available talent.

[4] The author wishes to thank Robert Kendall for his advice and counsel on the Pittsford situation.

[5] AnnaLee Saxenian, "Regional Networks and the Resurgence of the Silicon Valley", California Management Review 1990, pages 89-112.

[6] ibid page 91

[7] the German Baden-Wurtemmburg region is cited.

[8] Saxenian, op cit page 95

[9] ibid page 99

[10] ibid . page 96

[11] ibid page 97

[12] ibid page 98

[13] ibid page 10

[14] "An Exchange of Views on 'The Great Speckled Bird'" Educational Researcher,24,
    September 1995, 22-27

[15] ibid page 24

Regents Diploma and College Bound Intention "Close" Districts

District	County	1992	1993	1994
Bethlehem	Albany	59/83		60/84
Guilderland	Albany			57/87
Green Island	Albany		57/78	
Voorheesville	Albany		54/82	60/84
Chenango Forks	Broome	58/89		
Maine Endwell	Broome		65/78	
Alleghany	Cattaragus			56/81
Union Springs	Cayuga		58/76	
Bemus Point	Chautaugua		54/78	
Clymer	Chautaugua			57/75
Cortland	Cortland		56/80	59/83
Red Hook	Dutchess		57/84	
Spackenkill	Dutchess		58/80	
Rhinebeck	Dutchess			63/75
•Amherst	Erie			56/95
East Aurora	Erie		55/75	
Frontier	Erie		56/77	
Hamburg	Erie			56/85
Orchard Park	Erie		55/94	
Williamsville	Erie	57/92		
Newcomb	Essex	55/81		
Keene	Essex			66/75
Westport	Essex			68/75
Northville	Fulton		60/78	
Elba	Genesee			55/84
Long Lake	Hamilton		66/75	
Webb	Herkimer		71/74	
Lowville	Lewis			64/75
Avon	Livingston		58/76	
Caledonia-Mumford	Livingston			56/90

District	County	1992	1993	1994
Cazenovia	Madison			56/81
Churchville-Chili	Monroe			55/80
East Rochester	Monroe		54/82	
Fairport	Monroe		56/92	57/89
Gates Chili	Monroe			55/78
Penfield	Monroe			59/88
Spencerport	Monroe		58/79	
Webster	Monroe		55/85	57/85
Bellmore-Merrick	Nassau		59/91	
•East Williston	Nassau		59/92	
Hewlett-Woodbury	Nassau			55/95
Hicksville	Nassau		56/86	
Locust Valley	Nassau		54/84	
Oceanside	Nassau		57/96	
Port Washington	Nassau		56/94	
•Rockville Ctr	Nassau		58/96	
Seaford	Nassau			58/94
Starpoint	Niagara		56/86•	
Clinton	Oneida	59/89	54/83	59/83
•New Hartford	Oneida	58/89		
Sauquoit Valley	Oneida			54/79
Baldwinville	Onondaga		61/77	
Liverpool	Onondaga	59/87	58/87	54/8
Marcellus	Onondaga			57/92
Solvay	Onondaga	55/84		
Tully	Onondaga	57/87	59/97	
Canandaigua	Ontario			57/81
East Bloomfield	Ontario			64/75
Gorham-Middlesex	Ontario		56/75	54/78
Victor	Ontario	56/82	57/84	
Warwick Valley	Orange		57/79	
Cooperstown	Ostego		59/90	
Milford	Ostego		62/75	
Richfield Springs	Ostego	54/86		

District	County	1992	1993	1994
Oneonta	Ostego			54/87
East Greenbush	Rensselaer	57/81	55/80	59/83
Schodack	Rensselaer		55/81	
Clarkstown	Rockland	55/86		
Ramapo	Rockland	54/85		
Pearl River	Rockland			54/91
Madrid-Washington	St. Lawrence	72/64		
Canton	St. Lawrence		58/83	54/82
Ogdenburg	St. Lawrence			54/79
Burnt Hills	Saratoga	56/75	56/88	
Niskayuna	Schenectady	55/89	57/89	56/94
Cobleskill	Schoharie	58/85		
Amityville	Suffolk	56/86		
Commack	Suffolk	59/91	55/96	
Harborfields	Suffolk	58/93		55/97
Mattituck	Suffolk		54/89	56/88
•Mt. Sinai	Suffolk			59/89
Northport	Suffolk	54/86	55/88	58/86
Sayville	Suffolk		59/88	54/87
Shorham-Wading	Suffolk		56/93	
Smithtown	Suffolk	54/85		58/89
Southold	Suffolk	57/89		
Westhamption Bch	Suffolk	56/85	54/84	56/85
Liberty	Sullivan	56/74		
Ithaca	Tompkins		54/88	
New Paltz	Ulster			58/82
Queensbury	Warren		56/75	59/79
Glen Falls	Warren			54/80
Salem	Washington			57/79
Palmyra-Macedon	Wayne	55/77	58/81	
•Wayne	Wayne	56/80		
Williamson	Wayne			54/79

District	County	1992	1993	1994
•Briarcliff Manor	Westchester			58/93
Croton Harmon	Westchester	54/93		
Hasting/Hudson	Westchester	56/92	58/89	
•Pleasantville	Westchester		57/98	
Rye	Westchester			56/95
Yorktown	Westchester			58/93

• = Final 33 "Bulls-Eye" Districts

Regents Global Studies Course "Close " Districts

District	County	1992	1993	1994
Ravena-Coeyman	Albany		89/79	
Belmont	Alleghany	79/95		
Scio	Alleghany			84/76
Chenango Valley	Broome		79/95	
Deposit	Broome			77/83
Susquehanna Val	Broome			76/93
Union-Endicott	Broome	77/92		
Alleghany	Cattaragus	76/94		
Ellicottville	Cattaragus		78/79	
Randolph	Cattaragus			77/98
Port Bryan	Cattaragus			79/78
Moravia	Cayuga	99/78		
Dunkirk	Chautaugua			84/79
Mayville	Chautauqua	75/91		
Panama	Chautaugua		105/78	
Westfield	Chautauqua	77/93		77/76
Oxford	Chenango	94/79		
Sherburne	Chenango	99/76		76/96
Beekmantown	Clinton		77/92	
Homer	Cortland		76/83	78/81
McGraw	Cortland		79/87	
Andes	Delaware			77/100
Stamford	Delaware	79/78		
Walton	Delaware			98/75
Millbrook	Dutchess	82/78		
Northeast	Dutchess		76/81	75/96
Red Hook	Dutchess		78/98	
Pawling	Dutchess			77/84
Spackenkill	Dutchess		79/100	76/95
Cleveland Hill	Erie			75/88
Kenmore	Erie	77/81	92/79	
Grand Island	Erie		77/83	
Sloan-Maryvale	Erie	83/77	93/75	77/81
West Seneca	Erie			91/78
Elizabethtown	Essex			93/77
Lake Placid	Essex			95/76
Ticonderoga	Essex		81/78	84/77
Chateaugay	Franklin			79/83
Batavia	Genesee			79/85
Byron Bergen	Genesee	79/79		
Oakfield	Genesee		77/92	78/97

District	County	1992	1993	1994
Mohawk	Herkimer		93/76	
Lyme	Jefferson	127/79		
Carthage	Jefferson		95/75	
Thousand Island	Jefferson	79/82		
Caledonia	Livingston	77/88		75/93
Avon	Livingston	76/96		
Brookfield	Madison	106/79		
Cazenovia	Madison	78/86		91/79
DeRuyter	Madison	84/75		
Brighton	Monroe	79/91		
Brockport	Monroe			87/76
Fairport	Monroe			78/89
Gates-Chili	Monroe			78/91
Honeoye Falls	Monroe	77/91		76/94
Penfield	Monroe	79/95		
Rush Henretta	Monroe			93/78
Spencerport	Monroe		78/76	94/77
•W. Irondequoit	Monroe	76/93		
Wheatland-Chili	Monroe			78/80
Bellmore-Merrick	Nassau			75/100
East Meadow	Nassau			79/81
Farmingdale	Nassau	83/77		
•Great Neck	Nassau		77/95	
•Herricks	Nassau		79/92	
Oceanside	Nassau		79/89	
•Roslyn	Nassau		78/94	
Hicksville	Nassau	75/89		
Island Trees	Nassau	79/86		
Locust Valley	Nassau	76/94		
•Manhasset	Nassau	79/96		
North Shore	Nassau	91/76		
Seaford	Nassau	81/79	78/82	
Niagara Wheat	Niagara	78/81	79/83	
•Clinton	Oneida	78/83		
Sauquoit Valley	Oneida		78/91	
Fabius-Pompey	Onondaga	78/80		
•Jamesville-DeWitt	Onondaga	77/95		
•Skaneateles	Onondaga	78/92		
Solvay	Onondaga			76/80
West Genessee	Onondaga	79/88		
Liverpool	Onondaga		87/78	
Canandaigua	Ontario			78/88
East Bloomfield	Ontario	83/77		

District	County	1992	1993	1994
Gorham-Middle	Ontario			78/80
Highland Falls	Orange	77/86		86/79
Monroe-Woodmere	Orange			76/88
Valley-Montgom	Orange			83/78
Warwick Valley	Orange	77/95		
Altmar-Parrish	Oswego	90/76		92/76
Oswego	Oswego	78/85		84/79
Pulaski	Oswego	97/76		
Laurens	Ostego		90/79	
Oneonta	Ostego		77/79	
Mohopac	Putnam			94/78
Averill Park	Rensselaer	79/86		
Brunswick	Rensselaer		91/77	109/79
Nyack	Rockland	79/75		77/81
S. Orangetown	Rockland			78/91
Canton	St. Lawrence	78/90		
Colton-Pierpoint	St. Lawrence			97/79
Hammond	St. Lawrence	123/78		
Madrid Wadd	St. Lawrence		78/85	
Morristown	St. Lawrence		97/77	
Potsdam	St. Lawrence			79/97
Cornith	Saratoga	75/94		
Burnt Hills	Saratoga		78/86	
South Glen Falls	Saratoga			76/85
Schalmont	Schenectady		77/88	
Watkins Glen	Schuyler	77/90		
Hornell	Steuben	80/79		
Avoca	Steuben		96/77	85/77
Bayport-Blue	Suffolk			79/88
Connetquot	Suffolk	77/82	78/81	
Deer Park	Suffolk		79/91	
East Islip	Suffolk		77/78	
Eastport	Suffolk			76/98
Harborfields	Suffolk			79/94
•Half Hollow Hill	Suffolk	79/92		
Huntington	Suffolk			75/96
Islip	Suffolk	79/84		
Mattituck	Suffolk	75/82		
North Babylon	Suffolk			79/82
•Port Jefferson	Suffolk		79/89	77/97
Rocky Point	Suffolk	76/89		77/83
Sayville	Suffolk			79/81
South Huntington	Suffolk	75/88		76/94

District	County	1992	1993	1994
Southold	Suffolk		79/82	
•Three Village	Suffolk	92/77		79/91
West Islip	Suffolk	77/85		
William Floyd	Suffolk	79/77	77/82	83/78
Delaware Valley	Sullivan			76/79
Eldred	Sullivan	77/100		
Narrowsburg	Sullivan	78/83		79/87
Jeeff-Youngville	Sullivan	81/77		
Roscoe	Sullivan	77/80		
Owego-Apalachia	Tioga		78/80	
Groton	Tompkins	79/84		
Trumansburg	Tompkins			78/85
Marlboro	Ulster	77/80		
Hadley-Luzurne	Warren			87/75
North Warren	Warren		98/78	
Newark	Wayne			77/82
Greenwich	Washington	78/82		
•Ardsley	Westchester			77/97
•Briarcliff Manor	Westchester	79/93		78/87
Dobbs Ferry	Westchester			78/98
Eastchester	Westchester	79/88		
Hendrick Hudson	Westchester			78/80
Mamaroneck	Westchester	76/89		79/88
Lakeland	Westchester	88/76		
Rye	Westchester			79/100
Somers	Westchester	77/91		
Tuckahoe	Westchester	113/79		
Scarsdale	Westchester		79/93	

• = 33 Bulls-Eye Districts

Regents History/Government "Close " Course Districts

District	County	1992	1993	1994
Guilderland	Albany	75/92		
•North Colonie	Albany	76/94	77/94	
Belfast	Alleghany			76/96
Belmont	Alleghany			
Scio	Alleghany			109/76
Little Valley	Cattaragus			77/83
Union Springs	Cayuga		79/83	84/78
Clymer	Chautaugua	102/76		
Panama	Chautaugua			110/77
Plattsburgh	Clinton	81/79	78/82	78/82
Copake-Taconic	Columbia			84/76
Chatham	Columbia	90/77	91/77	
Homer	Cortland			75/86
Delhi	Delaware		77/92	
Sidney	Delaware	74/87		77/92
South Kortright	Delaware	104/79		
Red Hook	Dutchess	74/100		
Rhinebeck	Dutchess		78/97	
Spackenkill	Dutchess		79/99	
Clarence	Erie			105/77
East Aurora	Erie	77/94		95/79
Eden	Erie	78/96		
Frontier	Erie		75/88	
Sloan-Maryvale	Erie			96/74
West Seneca	Erie			84/79
Williamsville	Erie			77/92
Keene	Essex		78/100	
Tupper Lake	Franklin	81/76		
Pembroke	Genesee			76/83
Bridgewater	Herkimer	75/87		
Mohawk	Herkimer	91/77		88/78
W.Canada Valley	Herkimer	92/78		101/79
General Brown	Jefferson	78/92		85/77
Lyme	Jefferson	77/85		
LaFargeville	Jefferson		74/91	
Sacketts Harbor	Jefferson	108/77	85/77	
Carthage	Jefferson		74/89	
Beaver River	Lewis			77/96
Copenhagen	Lewis		79/89	
Lowville	Lewis		77/92	77/82
Avon	Livingston	79/78		
Caledonia-Mum	Livingston	78/86		

District	County	1992	1993	1994
E. Rochester	Monroe	75/93		79/93
Penfield	Monroe	75/94	79/94	
Spencerport	Monroe			97/77
•W. Irondequoit	Monroe		77/95	78/92
Wheatland Chili	Monroe	75/87		
Fort Plain	Montgomery			79/76
Bellmore-Merrick	Nassau	75/87		
Bethpage	Nassau	86/79		90/79
Carle Place	Nassau			100/76
Farmingdale	Nassau		84/79	
•Great Neck	Nassau	78/88	75/98	78/92
Hicksville	Nassau			75/87
•Herricks	Nassau			79/94
Island Trees	Nassau		75/90	
Lawrence	Nassau			79/96
Lynbrook	Nassau	78/82		
Massapequa	Nassau		79/87	
•Manhasset	Nassau		77/98	
Oceanside	Nassau		79/85	
Plainview	Nassau		75/96	
•Rockville Center	Nassau	79/88		
•Roslyn	Nassau			75/96
Wantagh	Nassau		78/97	
Adirondack	Oneida	77/95		
•Clinton	Oneida	78/98	75/94	
Westmoreland	Oneida		78/88	84/77
Baldwinsville	Onondaga		77/78	
•Fayetteville-Man.	Onondaga	76/95		
Liverpool	Onondaga			74/91
Onondaga	Onondaga	76/78		
West Genessee	Onondaga			79/90
East Bloomfield	Ontario		77/86	
Cornwall	Orange		78/90	
Goshen	Orange			79/85
Pine Bush	Orange	75/84		
Milford	Ostego	97/79		
Oneonta	Ostego		76/99	
Mahopac	Putnam		75/93	76/87
Clarkstown	Rockland	78/94	79/91	76/92
Pearl River	Rockland	76/86		
Nanuet	Rockland			77/94
Nyack	Rockland			78/87
Colton-Pierpoint	St. Lawrence			114/76
Madrid Wadding	St. Lawrence		76/89	

District	County	1992	1993	1994
Morristown	St. Lawrence			79/81
Burnt Hills	Saratoga		77/93	78/87
Mechanicville	Saratoga		76/82	
Shenendehowa	Saratoga	77/94	74/90	
Niskayuna	Schenectady	76/93		
Connetquot	Suffolk			74/83
Central Morchies	Suffolk	79/86		
•Cold Spring Harb	Suffolk	78/95		
Commack	Suffolk	79/92		
Comsewogue	Suffolk	76/82		
•Elwood	Suffolk			74/95
East Islip	Suffolk			77/86
Greenport	Suffolk	74/100		86/79
•Half Hollow Hill	Suffolk		78/93	
Huntington	Suffolk			75/90
•Kings Park	Suffolk			78/91
Mattituck	Suffolk	76/99		
Northport	Suffolk		78/94	
Rocky Point	Suffolk	75/89		77/87
Sachem	Suffolk			76/82
Sag Harbor	Suffolk		78/94	
Sayville	Suffolk	77/99	78/95	76/90
Shorham-Wading	Suffolk			76/91
Smithtown	Suffolk			79/93
South Huntington	Suffolk	75/96		
Southhampton	Suffolk	78/98	74/98	
Southold	Suffolk		78/98	
•Three Village	Suffolk			76/94
William Floyd	Suffolk			74/80
Eldred	Sullivan	77/100		
Roscoe	Sullivan		76/100	
Owego-Apalachin	Tioga		77/93	
Marlboro	Ulster		74/79	
New Paltz	Ulster		78/92	
Onteora	Ulster		77/89	
Hadley-Luzurne	Warren			78/78
Lake George	Warren	77/91		75/89
Lyons	Wayne	75/85		
Cambridge	Washington			84/79
•Ardsley	Westchester		78/100	
•Bryam Hills	Westchester			76/94
Mamaroneck	Westchester	76/91		74/91
Lakeland	Westchester	77/80	81/78	
•Pelham	Westchester	79/93		
Rye	Westchester			77/84
Somers	Westchester			78/91

District	County	1992	1993	1994
Tuckahoe	Westchester	75/83		
Valhalla	Westchester			75/80
Dundee	Yates			75/96

• = 33 Bulls-Eye Districts

Regents French "Close" Districts

District	County	1992	1993	1994
Harpursville	Broome	37/93		
Southern Cayuga	Cayuga		35/92	
Brocton	Chautaugua		37/100	
Falconer	Chautaugua	37/89		
Pine Valley	Chautaugua	38/81		
Elmira Heights	Chemung	35/100		
Norwich	Chenango	35/98		
Chatham	Columbia			35/100
Millbrook	Dutchess			39/100
Spackenkill	Dutchess		39/100	
Iroquois	Erie			36/97
Crown Point	Essex		38/100	
Elizabethtown	Essex		39/82	
Willsboro	Essex	36/89		
Chateaugay	Franklin	38/100		
Malone	Franklin			36/96
Saranac Lake	Franklin		35/90	
Northville	Fulton		39/91	35/100
Indian Lake	Hamilton	38/100		
Geneseo	Livingston		35/100	
Harrisville	Lewis	38/100		
Brokfield	Madison			35/86
•Pittsford	Monroe	35/96		
New York Mills	Oneida	37/100		
East Bloomfield	Ontario	36/86		
Geneva	Ontario			39/98
Naples	Ontario	38/92		
Altmar Parrish	Oswego	38/87		
Laurnes	Ostego			37/100
Morris	Ostego		38/100	
Richfield Spring	Ostego			37/95
Hammond	St. Lawrence		38/100	
Morristown	St. Lawrence			35/83
Ballston Spa	Saratoga		35/96	
Stillwater	Saratoga	37/79		
Duanesburg	Schenectady	38/100		
Jefferson	Schoharie		35/83	
Eastport	Suffolk		37/100	
Sayville	Suffolk		36/96	
Ithaca	Tompkins	38/97		

District	County	1992	1993	1994
New Paltz	Ulster		38/92	
North Warren	Warren	39/94		
Argyle	Washington	37/88		
Fort Ann	Washington			39/94
Gananada	Wayne	37/93		
•Ardsley	Westchester			37/100
Blind Brook	Westchester	39/100		
Croton Harmon	Westchester		36/100	38/100
Attica	Wyoming	38/98		

• = 33 Bulls-Eye Districts

Regents Spanish "Close " Districts

District	County	1992	1993	1994
Bethlehem	Albany	34/98	38/99	
Guilderland	Albany	35/100		
Green Island	Albany		35/100	
South Colonie	Albany	37/100	36/99	
Voorheesville	Albany	35/100		
Alfred Almond	Alleghany	35/95	37/84	35/100
Andover	Alleghany		36/100	
Belfast	Alleghany	35/92		
Cuba-Rushford	Alleghany			36/100
Canaserega	Alleghany		38/100	
Wellsville	Alleghany		35/94	
Chenango Forks	Broome	37/89	36/88	
Vestal	Broome		38/93	
Randolph	Cattaragus	37/93		
Limestone	Cattaragus			35/100
Cato Meridan	Cayuga	37/94		
Union Springs	Cayuga		38/81	
Bemus Point	Chautaugua			39/96
Falconer	Chautaugua	35/95	35/91	
Jamestown	Chautaugua			38/94
Mayville	Chautaugua			38/100
Ripley	Chautaugua	36/100		37/92
Georgn-S. Ostelic	Chenango		38/92	
New Berlin	Chenango	35/94		
South New Berlin	Chenango	39/100		
Norwich	Chenango	39/97		
Sherburne-Earlvi	Chenango			36/95
New Lebanon	Columbia			38/94
Germantown	Columbia	35/94		
Marathon	Cortland			37/88
Sidney	Delaware			36/83
Hyde Park	Dutchess		35/82	36/91
Pawling	Dutchess		39/96	
Spackenkill	Dutchess			38/100
Alden	Erie	36/92		
•Amherst	Erie	39/95		
Cheektowaga	Erie	39/93		
Cleveland Hill	Erie		35/100	
DePew	Erie			36/99
Eden	Erie		36/86	35/96
Hamburg	Erie		35/99	

District	County	1992	1993	1994
Orchard Park	Erie	36/99		
Sweet Home	Erie			36/93
West Seneca	Erie			35/90
Williamsville	Erie		35/95	
Tupper Lake	Franklin		38/93	37/97
Johnstown	Fulton	35/98		38/100
Mayfield	Fulton		39/83	
Alexander	Genesee			36/100
Oakfield	Genesee	36/100		
Pavilion	Genesee	36/96		36/93
Hunter-Tannersvi	Greene			39/100
Mohawk	Herkimer	35/100	39/91	
General Brown	Jefferson		39/99	
Carthage	Jefferson	35/98		
Beaver River	Lewis		38/100	
Lowville	Lewis		38/100	
Avon	Livingston		35/85	
Caledonia-Mumfo	Livingston		38/82	36/96
Geneseo	Livingston	37/92		37/88
Mt. Morris	Livingston		39/80	
Cazenovia	Madison	36/100	37/100	35/100
Chittenango	Madison	35/98		35/95
De Ruyter	Madison	39/79		
Brighton	Monroe		37/97	37/99
E. Irondequoit	Monroe	36/93		
E. Rochester	Monroe		36/94	
Gates Chili	Monroe	38/93	36/89	
Greece	Monroe		35/91	
Honeoye Falls	Monroe	38/88		
Penfield	Monroe	39/94		
Spencerport	Monroe	35/92		
Webster	Monroe	38/89	37/95	37/94
Amsterdam	Montgomery		38/94	35/96
Baldwin	Nassau	39/98		39/99
East Meadow	Nassau	36/98	37/96	
East Rockaway	Nassau	39/93		
Hicksville	Nassau			38/94
Island Trees	Nassau		37/85	
Locust Valley	Nassau	38/96		
Long Beach	Nassau	38/98		35/97
Lynbrook	Nassau		35/98	35/100
Malverne	Nassau	35/98		
District	County	1992	1993	1994
Oceanside	Nassau		37/100	

Port Washington	Nassau	39/100	38/100	
Uniondale	Nassau	37/93	39/78	39/96
West Hempstead	Nassau			35/99
Barker	Niagara		38/83	37/100
North Tonowanda	Niagara			35/92
Royalton Hartland	Niagara		37/84	
Starpoint	Niagara	38/96		
Holland Patent	Oneida	38/92		
•New Hartford	Oneida		36/99	38/96
Oriskany	Oneida		39/95	
Sherrill	Oneida	36/93		
Waterville	Oneida	36/96	38/100	
•Jamesville-Dewit	Onondaga		37/100	
North Syracuse	Onondaga		39/93	
West Genesee	Onondaga			36/99
•Westhill	Onondaga	37/98		
Geneva	Ontario	37/91		36/97
Naples	Ontario	35/87		38/96
Victor	Ontario		38/93	
Goshen	Orange			35/83
Highland Falls	Orange		35/100	37/98
Middletown	Orange			39/97
Minisink Valley	Orange	38/98	35/97	
Monroe Woodbur	Orange	35/98		
Pine Bush	Orange		39/84	
Washingtonville	Orange		36/93	
Holley	Orleans	36/100	39/97	38/100
Kendall	Orleans	39/96		36/89
Milford	Ostego		38/91	
Laurens	Ostego	35/100		
Oneonta	Ostego			36/98
Carmel	Putnam	38/100		
Mahopac	Putnam			36/96
Schodack	Rensselaer	39/100		36/100
Clarkstown	Rockland		37/99	
Haverstraw	Rockland		39/97	
East Ramapo	Rockland		39/97	
Pearl River	Rockland		36/96	
Nanuet	Rockland	37/100		
Nyack	Rockland	38/95		
Ramapo	Rockland	38/96		
Madrid Waddingt	St. Lawrence			36/95
Norwood-Norfolk	St. Lawrence			35/94
Ogdenburg	St. Lawrence	39/97		

District	County	1992	1993	1994
Parishville-Hopkin	St. Lawrence			36/100
Shenendehowa	Saratoga		38/98	
Schalmont	Schenectady			36/97
Gilboa-Conesville	Schoharie			37/92
Middleburgh	Schoharie	35/100		35/97
Canisteo	Steuben			35/100
Hammondsport	Steuben		39/89	
Prattsburgh	Steuben			39/100
Amityville	Suffolk	35/80		37/98
Copiague	Suffolk		35/93	
Connetquot	Suffolk			36/95
East Hampton	Suffolk		35/98	
Harborfields	Suffolk	38/99	38/100	36/100
Hauppauge	Suffolk	35/97	37/96	
Longwood	Suffolk	35/94		
•Mt. Sinai	Suffolk		36/98	
Shorham-Wading	Suffolk	35/100		36/100
South Country	Suffolk	37/95		38/85
West Babylon	Suffolk		35/93	
West Islip	Suffolk			36/97
Livingston Manor	Sullivan	37/100		39/89
Narrowsburg	Sullivan	35/100		
Tri Valley	Sullivan		38/96	
Waverly	Tioga		39/92	
Lansing	Tompkins	37/100		
Trumansburg	Tompkins			38/100
Ellenville	Ulster	39/100		
Highland	Ulster		36/98	
Queensbury	Warren			37/99
Granville	Washington		39/98	
Salem	Washington	36/84	38/94	36/80
Lyons	Wayne	37/89		
Newark	Wayne	38/79		
•Wayne	Wayne		38/90	
•Ardsley	Westchester			38/100
Bedford	Westchester	35/100		
Eastchester	Westchester		35/100	
Edgemont	Westchester		35/100	
Elmsford	Westchester		35/86	
Harrison	Westchester			39/93
Hasting onHudson	Westchester		36/100	
Irvington	Westchester		37/100	
Mt. Pleasant	Westchester		35/98	
Ossining	Westchester	36/99		

District	County	1992	1993	1994
Port Chester	Westchester		39/99	
Rye Neck	Westchester			35/100
Valhalla	Westchester		37/94	
Yorktown	Westchester	35/100	38/94	
Attica	Wyoming		36/98	
Warsaw	Wyoming	37/100		

• = 33 Bulls-Eye
Districts

Regents Intermediate Mathematics "Close" Districts

District	County	1992	1993	1994
Bethlehem	Albany		78/95	
Alfred Almond	Alleghany			78/79
Canaseraga	Alleghany			81/76
Maine Endwell	Broome	78/87		80/75
Vestal	Broome	75/81	77/80	
Portville	Cattaragus	79/83	76/84	
Southern Cayuga	Cayuga		77/91	
Pine Valley	Chautaugua		82/72	
Westfield	Chautaugua		76/78	
Mayville	Chautaugua			79/74
Greene	Chenango			79/78
Chatham	Columbia		76/84	
Copkae-Tacon	Columbia			81/74
Andes	Delaware			77/80
Stamford	Delaware			79/84
Delhi	Delaware	79/75		
Spackenkill	Dutchess		77/88	92/79
Alden	Erie	75/82		73/92
•Amherst	Erie	79/86		
Clarence	Erie			75/83
East Aurora	Erie		74/82	75/89
Eden	Erie		74/78	
Frontier	Erie		74/81	77/82
Hamberg	Erie			79/81
Iroquois	Erie		79/90	
West Seneca	Erie		77/73	79/76
Keene	Essex			75/100
Schroon Lake	Essex		79/84	
Westport	Essex	81/76		
Tupper Lake	Franklin		75/78	
Catskill	Greene			74/95
Mohawk	Herkimer	79/91		
Herkimer	Herkimer			78/86
Webb	Herkimer	92/78		
West Canada Val	Herkimer		79/93	
Indian River	Jefferson	86/79		
LaFargeville	Jefferson		74/96	
Genesso	Livingston	75/81	79/86	
York	Livingston			75/95
Copenhagen	Lewis		77/81	
Cazenovia	Madison		77/98	75/92
Brighton	Monroe	79/92	78/88	

District	County	1992	1993	1994
East Rochester	Monroe		93/75	
Fairport	Monroe		78/88	74/90
Gates Chili	Monroe	75/84	86/78	79/77
•Pittsford	Monroe	77/90	79/94	
Spencerport	Monroe			84/77
Wheatland Chili	Monroe	77/89		
Fonda-Fulton	Montgomery			78/88
Bellmore-Merrick	Nassau	91/75	91/74	96/73
Bethpage	Nassau			76/86
•East Williston	Nassau		77/95	
Farmingdale	Nassau			74/75
•Great Neck	Nassau		80/79	90/77
Hewlett-Wood	Nassau			76/97
Hicksville	Nassau			77/80
Levittown	Nassau		75/89	
•Manhasset	Nassau		75/89	
North Shore	Nassau		74/85	73/84
Plainview	Nassau	78/91	76/89	
•Rockville Centre	Nassau		76/90	79/90
•Roslyn	Nassau		77/94	
•Syosset	Nassau		106/78	
Seaford	Nassau	78/74		
Newfane	Niagara	90/76		
Starpoint	Niagara		77/93	73/92
•Clinton	Oneida			78/83
•New Hartford	Oneida	74/83	78/79	
New York Mills	Oneida		74/87	
Remsen	Oneida			78/80
Sauquoit Valley	Oneida			78/85
Fabius-Pompey	Onondaga			79/86
•Fayetteville-Manl	Onondaga	74/98		
LaFayette	Onondaga			77/84
Marcellus	Onondaga	75/88		
Solvay	Onondaga			76/75
Tully	Onondaga		75/98	
•Westhill	Onondaga			77/92
East Bloomfield	Ontario			90/76
Geneva	Ontario			73/82
Manchester-Sht	Ontario	77/80		
Naples	Ontario			77/74
Honeoye	Ontario	75/93		
Gorham-Middle	Ontario		79/96	
Victor	Ontario			76/83
Highland Falls	Orange		76/74	76/74

District	County	1992	1993	1994
Monroe-Wood	Orange			81/77
Warwick Valley	Orange		79/80	77/82
Albion	Orleans	77/83		77/78
Pulsaki	Oswego			74/74
Edmeston	Ostego			82/78
Richfield Spring	Ostego			76/90
Cooperstown	Ostego		76/86	
Morris	Ostego		76/100	
Brunswick	Rensselaer		78/93	
Clarkstown	Rockland	79/92		
Nyack	Rockland			74/92
Ramapo	Rockland			77/92
Pearl River	Rockland		87/79	
Hammond	St. Lawrence		77/75	
Herman DeKalb	St. Lawrence		91/74	
Madrid Waddington	St. Lawrence		75/75	88/76
LIsbon	St. Lawrence			82/76
Potsdam	St. Lawrence	78/94		83/79
Galway	Saratoga	78/82		76/82
Shenendehowa	Saratoga	75/92		
Mechanicville	Saratoga		79/90	
Burnt Hills	Saratoga			73/91
Duanesburg	Schenectady			90/78
Niskayuna	Schenectady	74/92		76/95
Scotia-Glenville	Schenectady	75/92		
Cobleskill	Schoharie		77/79	
Watkins Glen	Schuyler		77/79	78/84
Romulus	Seneca			74/91
Cohocton	Steuben	75/100		
Greenwood	Steuben			74/82
Jasper-Troup	Steuben			79/87
Bayport-Blue	Suffolk			77/83
Connetquot	Suffolk		75/75	
•Elwood	Suffolk		78/81	
East Hampton	Suffolk	95/75		
•Half Hollow Hills	Suffolk	74/87	74/86	
Hampton Bays	Suffolk			77/80
Harborfields	Suffolk		76/90	76/90
•Kings Park	Suffolk		79/90	
Northport	Suffolk		76/91	
Rocky Point	Suffolk	79/89		73/95
Sayville	Suffolk	77/90	77/79	
Shelter Island	Suffolk		78/93	79/87

District	County	1992	1993	1994
Sachem	Suffolk		81/77	75/82
Southhold	Suffolk	79/76	76/82	103/75
Westhampton	Suffolk			78/92
Delaware Valley	Sullivan			74/86
Tri Valley	Sullivan			79/94
Dryden	Tompkins		78/76	
Trumansburg	Tompkins			100/77
Lake George	Warren			91/76
Argyle	Washington			79/85
Cambridge	Washington		77/92	
Granville	Washington		76/89	
Gananda	Wayne			100/78
•Ardsley	Westchester		79/91	
Blind Brook	Westchester		75/97	
•Briarcliff Manor	Westchester		78/97	
Chappeaqua	Westchester	76/96		
Hendrix Hudson	Westchester			83/76
Irvington	Westchester		76/98	
Mamaroneck	Westchester			79/87
Mt. Pleasant	Westchester	74/90		
•Pelham	Westchester			77/88
Rye	Westchester	77/96		78/91

•= 33 Bulls-Eye Districts

Regents Advanced Mathematics "Close" Districts

District	County	1992	1993	1994
Guilderland	Albany	66/86		
•North Colonie	Albany	65/87		
Chenango Forks	Broome	63/84		68/79
Vestal	Broome	76/78	63/81	
Union Endicott	Broome		66/74	
Maine-Endwell	Broome			74/78
West Valley	Cattaragus		63/95	
Mayville	Chautaugua		78/68	
Silver Creek	Chautaugua			65/93
Afton	Chenango			65/76
Chazy	Clinton	62/95		
Chatham	Columbia	67/75		
McGraw	Cortland			70/79
Andes	Delaware	67/75		
Delhi	Delaware			65/88
Rhinebeck	Dutchess		65/94	
•Amherst	Erie			75/76
East Aurora	Erie	65/97		
Iroquois	Erie			65/85
Keene	Essex			63/80
W. Canada Valley	Herkimer			63/80
Genesso	Livingston	65/79		
Hamilton	Madison		74/74	
Cazenovia	Madison			67/73
Brighton	Monroe	79/91		
Fairport	Monroe	66/96	66/89	
•Pittsford	Monroe		63/92	
Spencerport	Monroe			65/81
Bellmore-Merrick	Nassau		65/89	
•Manhasset	Nassau	66/91		
•Herricks	Nassau			63/98
Levittown	Nassau			65/85
Plainview	Nassau			64/90
Pt. Washington	Nassau			63/90
North Shore	Nassau		65/85	
•Syosset	Nassau	64/94	66/93	

District	County	1992	1993	1994
•New Hartford	Oneida	65/91		65/84
La Fayette	Onondaga	64/88		
Fabius-Pompey	Onondaga			66/76
•Jamesville-Dewitt	Onondaga		75/78	63/91
Marcellus	Onondaga	64/86		
Solvay	Onondaga	65/91		
•Westhill	Onondaga		84/76	
Gorham-Middle	Ontario		66/93	
Warwick Valley	Orange			64/85
Cooperstown	Ostego		64/93	64/84
Mahopac	Putnam		66/86	
Brunswick	Rensselaer			66/94
Clarkstown	Rockland			66/92
Nanuet	Rockland	63/93		
Edward-Knox	St. Lawrence		65/79	
Morristown	St. Lawrence		65/75	
Burnt Hills	Saratoga	64/92		
Niskayuna	Schenectady		63/97	
Commack	Suffolk			64/91
•Elwood	Suffolk		64/92	66/84
Fishers Island	Suffolk	100/75		
•Half Hollow Hills	Suffolk	65/92		
Huntington	Suffolk			64/81
Mattituck	Suffolk	64/90		
•Mt. Sinai	Suffolk			72/79
Northport	Suffolk			64/88
•Port Jefferson	Suffolk	64/97	63/90	64/93
Shorham-Wading	Suffolk	65/95		
Shelter Island	Suffolk			70/78
•Three Village	Suffolk	66/87		71/79
West Islip	Suffolk	66/86		
Tioga	Tioga			63/100
Granville	Washington			63/86
•Wayne	Wayne			64/96
Blind Brook	Westchester		63/100	
•Byram Hills	Westchester	63/95		
Dobbs Ferry	Westchester		63/94	

District	County	1992	1993	1994
Irvington	Westchester		66/96	
Rye	Westchester			66/90

• = 33 Bulls-Eye Districts

Regents Biology "Close" Districts

District	County	1992	1994	1994
South Colonie	Albany	85/76		90/75
Whitesville	Alleghany			85/76
Chenango Forks	Broome		79/92	75/94
Johnson City	Broome		79/80	
Maine-Endwell	Broome			76/88
Vestal	Broome		77/91	
Port Byron	Cayuga			79/83
Union Springs	Cayuga			95/79
Weedsport	Cayuga		75/85	
Mayville	Chautaugua		76/95	
Panama	Chautaugua		95/76	
Silver Creek	Chautaugua		88/79	78/85
Southwestern	Chautaugua		77/80	
Westfield	Chautaugua	77/90		
Bainbridge	Chenango			78/84
Saranac	Clinton		79/77	
Chatham	Columbia		89/78	91/77
Andes	Delaware		77/100	
Delhi	Delaware		76/93	76/95
Sidney	Delaware		77/81	82/75
South Kortright	Delaware	86/72		
Arlington	Dutchess	78/86		
Pawling	Dutchess		77/81	77/48
Ticonderoga	Essex			76/91
Byron Bergen	Genesse	79/75		
Greenville	Greene	74/76		
Poland	Herkimer	75/88		
Mohawk	Herkimer	73/90		
Carthage	Jefferson	75/83		
General Brown	Jefferson	73/85		76/90
LaFargeville	Jefferson		77/88	
Thousand Is.	Jefferson	112/78		
Beaver River	Lewis			76/79
Copenhagen	Lewis	79/89		
Lowville	Lewis	77/78		
Caledonia	Livingston			79/87

District	County	1992	1993	1994
Geneseo	Livingston	76/95		79/84
De Ruyter	Madison	76/93		
Hamilton	Madison		79/76	
Oneida	Madison	77/83		
Fairport	Monroe	76/92	79/89	
Hilton	Monroe	75/87		
Honeoye-Falls	Monroe	75/91		
Penfield	Monroe			77/96
•Pittsford	Monroe	75/96		
Spencerport	Monroe	90/76		
Bellmore-Merr	Nassau	79/81	85/76	
Bethpage	Nassau			79/92
Carle Place	Nassau		79/93	
•East Willistone	Nassau		78/99	
Farmingdale	Nassau	78/80		
•Great Neck	Nassau		77/94	
•Herricks	Nassau	79/91		
Hewlett-Wood	Nassau	79/92	76/87	
Lawrence	Nassau		75/90	
•Manhasset	Nassau	78/96		
North Shore	Nassau			77/80
Oceanside	Nassau	84/78		
Plainview	Nassau		75/96	77/98
•Roslyn	Nassau			79/98
Seaford	Nassau	78/80	78/76	
Lewiston-Porter	Niagara		79/79	
Newfane	Niagara	78/81		
Camden	Oneida		75/88	75/87
Waterville	Oneida	73/85		
Baldwinsville	Onondaga			76/88
•Jamesville-De	Onondaga			75/83
LaFayette	Onondaga		76/87	
Marcellus	Onondaga	77/94		78/99
N. Syracuse	Onondaga		78/83	
Honeoye	Ontario	75/80		79/95
Naples	Ontario			77/95
Cornwall	Orange			79/88
Florida	Orange	92/76	76/79	

District	County	1992	1993	1994
Goshen	Orange	99/78		
Monroe-Woodb	Orange		75/90	
Albion	Orleans		78/76	
Holley	Orleans	77/79	93/77	
Kendall	Orleans			78/77
Fulton	Oswego			79/81
Mexico	Oswego		85/77	
Mahopac	Putnam	78/93		
Averill Park	Rensselaer	76/77		78/88
Brunswick	Rensselaer			87/78
Schodack	Rensselaer		77/88	77/88
Clarkstown	Rockland	77/90	78/94	
Ramapo	Rockland			78/90
Edward-Knox	St. Lawrence	75/79		76/81
Herman-DeKa	St. Lawrence			78/89
Madrid-Waddin	St. Lawrence	75/93		
Morristown	St. Lawrence			76/81
Potsdam	St. Lawrence	79/97		
Burnt Hills	Saratoga	79/90	83/75	77/93
Mechanicville	Saratoga	78/86		
S. Glen Falls	Saratoga			76/87
Scotia-Glenville	Schenectady		78/92	
Romulus	Seneca		194/76	
Seneca Falls	Seneca		107/76	
Jefferson	Schoharie			0/79
Cohocton	Steuben	75/92		
Jasper-Troupsb	Steuben	78/90		
Center Morich	Suffolk	84/76		
Commack	Suffolk	77/81		75/93
Comsewogue	Suffolk			84/79
East Hampton	Suffolk	86/75		
East Islip	Suffolk		77/79	
•Half Hollow H	Suffolk	79/87		
Hauppagauge	Suffolk	78/79		
•Kings Park	Suffolk	92/74		85/78
•Mt. Sinai	Suffolk			78/86
Sachem	Suffolk	84/74		79/76
Smithtown	Suffolk	80/79	81/78	76/85

District	County	1992	1993	1994
Southold	Suffolk	79/88		
•Three Village	Suffolk		78/93	77/92
West Babylon	Suffolk			77/80
Narrowsburg	Sullivan	86/78		
Newfield	Thompkins			75/78
New Paltz	Ulster		77/91	
Onteora	Ulster		75/95	
Queensbury	Warren	77/89		
Newark	Wayne			76/78
Cambridge	Washington	78/92		
•Ardsley	Westchester		78/93	
Blind Brook	Westchester		79/93	76/98
Bronxviille	Westchester		79/93	
Chappaqua	Westchester	73/98		
Croton Harmon	Westchester		96/75	
Hasting/Hudson	Westchester	76/92		
Katonah	Westchester			78/92
North Salem	Westchester			99/75
•Pleasantville	Westchester	76/97		
Rye	Westchester		75/95	77/91
Rye Neck	Westchester			77/80
Scarsdale	Westchester			75/98
Valhalla	Westchester	95/79		
Yorktown	Westchester		76/88	

• = 33 Bulls-
Eye Districts

Regents Chemistry "Close" Districts

District	County	1992	1993	1994
Belmont	Alleghany	64/89		
Maine Endwell	Broome			65/86
Alleghany	Cattaragus		64/92	
West Valley	Cattaragus		63/80	
Dunkirk	Chautaugua	66/85		
Chatham	Columbia		66/79	
Germantown	Columbia		65/83	
Rhinebeck	Dutchess	63/80		
East Aurora	Erie	66/79		
Eden	Erie		66/88	
Webb	Herkimer	64/81		
Geneseo	Livingston	74/75		
Mt. Morris	Livingston			66/97
Lowville	Lewis			63/94
DeRuyter	Madison			65/88
Brighton	Monroe		64/80	64/94
Penfield	Monroe	65/92	63/91	
•W. Irondequoit	Monroe	63/82	66/79	
Bellmore-Merr	Nassau		66/87	64/9
Hewlett Wood	Nassau		65/99	
•Manhasset	Nassau			64/96
North Shore	Nassau			63/95
Plainview	Nassau		65/90	
•Rockville Ctr.	Nassau	64/97		
•Syosset	Nassau	64/97		
Lewiston Porter	Niagara			64/81
New York Mills	Oneida			67/77
Morris	Ostego	69/75		
Mahopac	Putnam		66/93	
Clarkstown	Rockland	63/89	63/88	
Pearl River	Rockland	63/87		
S. Orangetown	Rockland		65/86	
Burnt Hills	Saratoga		63/84	
Niskayuna	Schenectady	63/90	66/88	64/94
Jefferson	Schoharie	93/79		
Mattituck	Suffolk	63/88		
North Babylon	Suffolk		66/84	

District	County	1992	1993	1994
Shorham-Wadi	Suffolk		65/91	
Southold	Suffolk			65/100
•Three Village	Suffolk		64/92	
Westhampton B	Suffolk		63/96	
New Paltz	Ulster		66/85	
Onteora	Ulster		65/87	
Fort Edwards	Washington			66/87
•Wayne	Wayne	65/86		
•Briarcliff Man	Westchester	65/98		
Bronxville	Westchester			65/94
Croton Harmon	Westchester			63/98
Elmsford	Westchester	71/76		
Harrison	Westchester			64/97
Hasting Hudson	Westchester	63/94		
Katonah-Lewis	Westchester	66/93		
•Pleasantville	Westchester	63/88		

Regents Physics "Close" Districts

District	County	1992	1993	1994
Bethlehem	Albany	36/97		34/93
•North Colonie	Albany	35/96	38/95	36/98
South Colonie	Albany		40/75	
Bolivar	Alleghany			35/83
Belfast	Alleghany		50/76	
Richburg	Alleghany		44/73	36/78
Maine Endwell	Broome		38/92	34/93
Vestal	Broome			37/80
Alleghany	Cattaragus			42/79
Ellicottville	Cattaragus		37/89	
Hinsdale	Cattaragus			36/100
Clymer	Chautagua		38/100	
Dunkirk	Chautagua		44/79	
Beekmantown	Clinton		34/90	
Chazy	Clinton		35/85	
Plattsburgh	Clinton			35/92
Saranac	Clinton		34/83	
New Lebanon	Columbia			36/93
South Kortright	Delaware	86/79		
Arlington	Dutchess		35/97	
•Amherst	Erie		38/90	
East Aurora	Erie			35/90
Grand Island	Erie	37/95		
Iroquois	Erie	37/93		
Minerva	Essex			36/100
Lake Placid	Essex	35/90		
Moriah	Essex		37/83	
Ticonderoga	Essex	37/81		
LeRoy	Genesee	35/94	35/88	
Mohawk	Herkimer			37/94
Van Hornesville	Herkimer			60/75
Webb	Herkimer	36/100		
LaFargeville	Jefferson			35/100
Lowville	Lewis	39/96		34/98
DeRuyter	Madison		39/93	38/100
Hamilton	Madison			39/82
Madison	Madison			37/80

District	County	1992	1993	1994
Fairport	Monroe		38/93	
Gates Chili	Monroe			37/94
•Pittsford	Monroe	34/100	38/97	
Spencerport	Monroe	37/95	37/82	
Wheatland Chili	Monroe	38/91		39/96
Baldwin	Nassau		36/90	
Bellmore-Merrick	Nassau			35/91
Hewlett-Woodmere	Nassau			39/94
•Roslyn	Nassau	39/83		
Niagara Wheatfield	Niagara			38/79
•Clinton	Oneida	37/95		39/98
•New Hartford	Oneida	37/89		
New York Mills	Oneida		36/95	
•FayettevilleManlius	Onondaga	37/99		
Layfayette	Onondaga	38/84	39/96	
Marcellus	Onondaga	36/96		39/93
•Skateateles	Onondaga		39/98	
West Genesee	Onondaga			34/99
•Westhill	Onondaga			37/92
Phelps- Clifton	Ontario			35/98
Geneva	Ontario		35/96	
Chester	Orange	36/100		
Monroe Woodbury	Orange		34/91	
Washingtonville	Orange	35/84		
Oneonta	Ostego	38/100		
Clarkstown	Rockland			38/97
Nanuet	Rockland			35/98
South Orangetown	Rockland		39/75	35/92
Potsdam	St. Lawrence		34/97	
Burnt Hills	Saratoga	34/93		
Galway	Saratoga	35/96		34/87
Scotia Glenville	Schenectady		35/93	36/100
Cobleskill-Richmond	Schoharie			37/89
Romulus	Seneca	37/100	37/88	38/98
Cohocton	Steuben		36/100	
Prattsburgh	Steuben	72/76		
East Islip	Suffolk		35/79	
Elwood	Suffolk			34/92
Greenport	Suffolk	37/81		

District	County	1992	1993	1994
•Half Hollow Hills	Suffolk	38/93	37/96	
Mattituck	Suffolk	36/92	35/90	
Northport	Suffolk			34/94
Shorham-Wading	Suffolk			34/96
Smithtown	Suffolk	35/95	35/92	
Southold	Suffolk	39/96		38/88
•Three Villages	Suffolk			39/91
West Islip	Suffolk		38/86	38/94
Westhampton Bch	Suffolk		37/96	
Groton	Tompkins		35/100	39/96
Lansing	Tompkins		36/80	38/81
Fort Edward	Washington			37/92
Gananda	Wayne	39/87		
Lyons	Wayne			37/93
Blind Brook	Westchester			37/100 ·
Chappeaqua	Westchester	34/90		38/91
Edgemont	Westchester	38/92	34/94	
Elmsford	Westchester			35/93
Katonah-Lewis	Westchester			35/100
Hastings on Hudson	Westchester		34/100	
Hendrix Hudson	Westchester	35/98		
Mamaroneck	Westchester	36/99	34/91	37/97
Rye	Westchester			35/96
Scarsdale	Westchester	35/100	38/99	
Tuckahoe	Westchester			37/95
Yorktown	Westchester		39/100	35/99
Letchworth	Wyoming	34/85		

• = 33 Bulls-Eye Districts

Districts Receiving "50 64" Variances Between January 1994 and June 1995

History/Global Studies		Biology		Math 1,2 & 3	
District	County	District	County	District	County
Casaserega	Alleghany	Canaserega	Alleghany	Ellicottville	Cattaragus
Cattaragus	Cattarags	Ellicottville	Cattarags	Amherst•	Erie
Ellicottville	Cattarags	Gowanda	Cattarags	Minerva	Essex
Franklinville	Cattarags	Pine Valley	Chautaug	Newcomb	Essex
Gowanda	Cattarags	Bainbridge	Chenango	Lowville	Lewis
Randolph	Cattarags	Oxford	Chenango	Mt. Morris	Livingston
Yorkshire-P	Cattarags	Norwich	Chenango	Wheatland	Monroe
Cassadagus	Chautaug	New Berlin	Chenango	Baldwin	Nassau
Falconer	Chautauq	Sherburne	Chenango	E. Meadow	Nassau
Panama	Chautauq	S. N. Berlin	Chenango	Uniondale	Nassau
Pine Valley	Chautauq	Delhi	Delaware	Canandagua	Ontario
Bainbridge	Chenango	Franklin	Delaware	Gorham	Ontario
Oxford	Chenango	Hancock	Delaware	Honeoye	Ontario
Norwich	Chenango	Sidney	Delaware	Manchester	Ontario
New Berlin	Chenango	Walton	Delaware	Phelps	Ontario
Sherburne	Chenango	Dover	Dutchess	Stillwater	Saratoga
S. N. Berlin	Chenango	Millbrook	Dutchess	Schalmont	Schenectady
Homer	Cortland	Poughkeep	Dutchess	Romulus	Seneca
Delhi	Delaware	Spackenkill	Dutchess	Waterloo	Seneca
Franklin	Delaware	Wappingers	Dutchess	Arkport	Steuben
Hancock	Delaware	*Amherst	Erie	West Islip	Suffolk
Margaretvil	Delaware	Hamburg	Erie	Argyle	Warren
Sidney	Delaware	Crown Point	Essex	Cambridge	Warren
S. Kortright	Delaware	Minerva	Essex	Fort Ann	Warren
Stamford	Delaware	Newcomb	Essex	Hartford	Warren
Walton	Delaware	Lake Placid	Essex	Salem	Warren
Dover	Dutchess	St. Regis Fal	Franklin	Clyde	Wayne
Millbrook	Dutchess	Tupper Lake	Franklin	Gananda	Wayne
Poughkeep	Dutchess	Johnstown	Fulton	Lyons	Wayne
Spackenkill	Dutchess	Alexander	Genesse	Marion	Wayne
Wappingers	Dutchess	Gen. Brown	Jefferson	North Rose	Wayne
Amherst•	Erie	Watertown	Jefferson	Sodus	Wayne
EvansBryant	Erie	Copenhagen	Lewis	Wayne•	Wayne
Kenmore-To	Erie	Lowville	Lewis	Williamson	Wayne
Crown Point	Essex	Geneseo	Livingstn	Briarcliff M	Westchester
Minerva	Essex	Mt. Morris	Livingstn	Lakeland	Westchester
Newcomb	Essex	Canastoga	Madison	North Salem	Westchester
Lake Placid	Essex	Morrisville	Madison	Peekskill	Westchester
St. Regis Fal	Franklin	Stockbridge	Madison	Yorktown	Westchester
Tupper Lake	Franklin	Baldwin	Nassau	Penn Yan	Yates
Broadalbum	Fulton	E.Rockaway	Nassau	Dundee	Yates
Johnstown	Fulton	Freeport	Nassua		

Global Stud/	History	Biology		Math 1,2&3
Mayfield	Fulton	Hicksville	Nassau	
Alexander	Genesse	Island Trees	Nassau	
Hunter-Tann	Greene	Rockville C	Nassau	
Alexandria	Jefferson	Uniondale	Nassau	
Carthage	Jefferson	Westbury	Nassau	
Gen.. Brown	Jefferson	Camden	Oneida	
LaFargeville	Jefferson	Sherrill	Oneida	
Watertown	Jefferson	Chester	Orange	
Copenhagen	Lewis	Florida	Orange	
Lowville	Lewis	Middletown	Orange	
South Lewis	Lewis	Minisink	Orange	
Dansville	Livingstn	Monroe-W	Orange	
Geneseo	Livingstn	Pine Bush	Orange	
Mt. Morris	Livingstn	Port Jervis	Orange	
Canastoga	Madison	Tuxedo	Orange	
Hamilton	Madison	Warwick Va	Orange	
Morrisville-	Madison	Albion	Orleans	
Stockbridge	Madison	Gilbertville-	Ostego	
Brockport	Monroe	Averill Park	Rensselae	
Greece	Monroe	Clarkstown	Rockland	
Hilton	Monroe	Stillwater	Saratoga	
Rush Henr	Monroe	Corning	Steuben	
Wheatland	Monroe	Owego-Ap	Steuben	
Baldwin	Nassau	Parrishville	St. Lawre	
E. Meadow	Nassau	Patchoque	Suffolk	
E.Rockaway	Nassau	Marlboro	Ulster	
Freeport	Nassau	Glen Falls	Warren	
Hicksville	Nassau	Johnsburg	Warren	
Island Trees	Nassau	N. Warren	Warren	
Rockville Cr	Nassau	Queensbury	Warren	
Uniondale	Nassau	Warrensbug	Warren	
Westbury	Nassau	Argyle	Washing	
Newfane	Niagara	Cambridge	Washing	
Niagara W	Niagara	Fort Ann	Washing	
North Tonn	Niagara	Hartford	Washing	
Royalton	Niagara	Salem	Washing	
Starpoint	Niagara	Briarcliff M	Westchest	
Adirondack-	Oneida	Lakeland	Westchest	
Camden	Oneida	N. Rochelle	Westchest	
Sherrill	Oneida	North Salem	Westchest	
Liverpool	Onondaga	Peekskill	Westchest	
Marcellus	Onondaga	Yorktown	Westchest	
Skateateles•	Onondaga	Warsaw	Wyoming	
Canandaiga	Ontario			
Gorham-M	Ontario			
Honeoye	Ontario			

Global Stud/	History
Manchester	Ontario
Naples	Ontario
Phelps	Ontario
Chester	Orange
Florida	Orange
Middletown	Orange
Monroe-W	Orange
Minisink	Orange
Pine Bush	Orange
Port Jervis	Orange
Tuxedo	Orange
Warwick Va	Orange
Albion	Orleans
Edmeston	Ostego
Gilbert-Mt.	Ostego
Laurens	Ostego
Milford	Ostego
Schenevus	Ostego
Altmar Par	Oswego
Central Sq.	Oswego
Fulton	Oswego
Hannibal	Oswego
Pulaski	Oswego
Sandy Creek	Oswego
Averill Park	Rensselae
Schodack	Rensselae
Clarkstown	Rockland
Parrishville	St. Lawre
Stillwater	Saratoga
Rotterdam	Schenec
Schalmont	Schenect
Gilboa-Cone	Schoharie
Schoharie	Schoharie
Romulus	Seneca
Waterloo	Seneca
Arkport	Steuben
Corning	Steuben
Hornell	Steuben
Lindenhurst	Suffolk
Patchoque-	Suffolk
*Three Villa	Suffolk
West Islip	Suffolk
Owego-Ap	Tioga
Marlboro	Ulster
Glen Falls	Warren
Johnsburg	Warren

Global Stud	History
N. Warren	Warren
Queensbury	Warren
Warrensbu	Warren
Argyle	Washing
Cambridge	Washing
Fort Ann	Washing
Hartford	Washing
Saelm	Washing
Clyde	Wayne
Gananda	Wayne
Lyons	Wayne
Marion	Wayne
North Rose	Wayne
Wayne•	Wayne
Williamson	Wayne
Ardsley•	Westchest
Briarcliffr•	Westchest
Dobbs Ferry	Westches
Hasting- Hu	Westches
Lakeland	Westches
N. Rochelle	Westches
North Salem	Westches
Ossining	Westches
Peekskill	Westcehst
Rye Neck	Westchest
Tuckahoe	Westchest
Valhalla	Westchest
Yorktown	Westchest
Warsaw	Wyoming
Dundee	Yates

• = 33
Bullseye
Districts

Index

Author Sketch

David Wiles has been a Professor of Educational Administration in the Department of Educational Administration and Policy Studies of the State University of New York since the 1978-1979 school year. His area of academic specialization is in educational politics, with special interests in rural policy and state wide restructuring efforts.

The author would be pleased to communicate with those interested in extending the calculation of Regents performance points and the combining of State Education Department and Office of Comptroller data sets. He can be reached through the publisher or through the Albany campus of the university. The Albany campus has proved to be an especially valuable location to conduct the kind of technical translating work incorporated in this work. During the past few years descriptive information presented here were utilized to help teach graduate seminars concerned with data driven program evaluation and give policy briefings to different state audiences on the politics of systematic assessment efforts.

Professor Wiles received his doctorate from the University of Florida in 1969 and has served on the faculty of the Ontario Institute for Studies in Education (University of Toronto), Virginia Polytechnic Institute and State University and Miami University (Ohio). He has written numerous articles on educational policy and has published texts in the areas of educational research, decision theory and the politics of school administration.

For the past three decades he has been married to Dr. Marilyn McCall Wiles, President of ALERT, and they have two grown sons, Corey and Matthew. The Wiles family can be found in either New York or the St. Augustine area of Florida.